L♥VE SELLING

how to sell without selling out

AUDREY CHAPMAN

RETHINK PRESS

First published in Great Britain 2016
by Rethink Press (www.rethinkpress.com)

© Copyright Audrey Chapman
Illustrations by Tim Kenning

For my

Mom and Dad, Pat and Dennis Wood.

Thank you.

Contents

Introduction

Almost every book about sales, majors on Closing – I want to start a conversation about Opening.

WARNING: If you want a book that has tons of hard core sales Closing techniques to batter your clients with, please go now. Don't read this. It's not for you.

This book is not about Closing or being Closed

It's about Opening and being Open.

If you're interested in starting a conversation about openness in sales, this is for you. If you're interested in how using open sales techniques can support an integrous and wholehearted approach to successful selling, then read on.

In the spirit of openness let me tell what this book will give you.

- It will show you how you can find and enhance a love for selling that is in complete alignment with who you are.

- It will open up your sales success as you root yourself in integrity.

- It will provide you with concepts and skills that complement a wholehearted sales process.

- Whilst letting go of any perceived fear, doubt and any uncertainty you may have, it'll provide you with a platform for your confidence to develop and grow.

- You will easily be able to let go of any sales embarrassment and just get down to delivering excellence.

- It will provide a process and structure that is based in values of true service, where you can and are expected to stay true to yourself and your values.

- It will encourage and push you to be authentic and stay authentic.

- You will identify what's holding you back, what's propelling you forward and let go of anything that's not serving the greater good of you and your clients.

- You'll be given many opportunities to consider how you may wish to adapt what you're already doing.

- You will be in a strong position to optimise your profit.

This is my invitation to you to join the conversation about Opening rather than getting stuck in Closing.

Above all, it's my invitation to you to fall hopelessly in love with selling.

This book is not for everyone. But, if you can tick one or more of the above boxes it is for you.

> *'Life isn't about finding yourself.*
> *Life is about creating yourself.'*

George Bernard Shaw

My sales life started when I was five-and-a-half years old.

I was the only child of Dennis and Pat Wood. We lived in the idyllic mountain side community called Llandudno, about seven miles south of Cape Town, South Africa. Like most kids of that age I never gave it any thought; it was just where we lived. It was home, where I went to school and where my friends and I would play with our dogs and ride our bikes.

The beach at Llandudno was and still is one that folk will travel miles to enjoy. The soft white sand is sublime and the huge Atlantic waves are a firm favourite for surfers. So each weekend it would fill to the brim with visitors.

A long day at the beach in the scorching heat often meant that people would leave their glass bottles of Coca-Cola half buried in the sand at the shore line. The Atlantic Ocean is pretty cold so it was a perfect place to keep drinks really cool until they wanted them.

That's when my sales career was launched.

I remember my excitement when one Sunday I discovered numerous bottles of icy cold Coca-Cola half buried in the sand at the shore line. Just right there; on my beach. It was especially exciting because Llandudno didn't have any shops, so no one would be able to buy a drink anywhere locally.

So I set up a small stall on the grass verge at the side of the beach, gathered all the bottles from the sea shore and in no time started selling drinks to the visitors. I trudged from from towel to towel asking people if they'd like to buy a bottle of Coca-Cola. Of course, they all bought; it was exactly what they wanted. I was thrilled. I guess I had found a product and had identified a market.

Boom! I was in business.

I had an absolutely fantastic day. My Cola was flying off my stall, money was rolling in and everyone seemed so happy.

Later that afternoon as the sun started to lose the full power of its heat I packed up and made my way home. As I went home with my stash of cash, I felt fantastic. I was a success. I was thrilled. I couldn't wait to tell my Dad.

My Dad had been in sales most of his life. He was an excellent salesman. I'm probably a little biased but to me he was and still is the most amazing sales person I've ever met. He loved selling, loved putting deals together and broking for others. His guiding value was that everyone was thrilled with the outcome. I felt sure that he'd be so proud of me when he knew of my sales success at the beach that day.

This became our family joke for years. He told the story time and time again about how his daughter first entered her sales career. How she had stolen the visitors' Coca-Cola bottles that they had carefully placed at the sea shore to keep chilled and then sold said Cola straight back to them.

I was lucky that everyone saw the funny side of my first sales enterprise, sweetly forgiving me for stealing their product and kind enough to buy it back from me at the going rate. I was fortunate that my entrepreneurship started when I was five-and-a-half, when stealing product could be met with smiles.

But I remember that day as though it was yesterday. It was such fun to be able to give something to someone that they really wanted and needed and it was a buzz for the fair exchange to be money.

I'm pleased to report that my days of stealing product and selling it back to the original owner were short lived but I'll never forget that day when my career in sales started.

Since then, whether helping customers find their perfect pair of jeans as a Sales Assistant in a jeans store, or being part of the excitement of a client's home refurbishment when I was a Showroom Manager for a home improvement store, it all still thrills me to this day. I love the whole process of helping the client create something uniquely beautiful for themselves – no matter what the product or service.

When I was promoted to my first sales management role, as an Area Sales Manager with the responsibility of managing thirty-six stores, I always found that the majority of folk really just wanted to do a great job for their customers. And when given the chance of knowing how to, they responded immediately by delivering excellent service which resulted in delighted customers.

It was my first senior management position with a FTSE Top 25 organisation that gave me the scope and structure to formalise what had previously worked for me in an organic way beforehand. Holding a position where I would be expected to lead, grow the business whist living the values of the brand, I was absolutely clear that I would do my best to over achieve in every possible way. Not only in the obvious business metrics but also through the softer targets of people management, employee engagement, collaboration and service excellence. Being a leader who led by example and from the front was hugely important to me. My management team and sales force of some 120 people stepped up to the plate and we built a business that was rooted in serving with delight. Growing our sales turnover from £50 million to over £100 million in a few years was an indicator that we were doing something right. It was a monumental joy.

So it was obvious to me that when I took up my first Sales Director role I knew that I not only had the scope but it was actually my responsibility to ensure that everyone in my function knew my thoughts on what good sales looked like. It was my duty to do whatever I could for us to be successful and over achieve whilst serving with grace.

Quite simply, putting clients at the centre of everything that you do in sales, works.

I've worked alongside some amazing folks over the years. Whether in my corporate roles, freelance and consulting projects, design and training assignments or my coaching practice and in my business today. There is seldom a day that passes where I don't thank my lucky stars that, having fallen in love with selling all those years ago, I still get to do it today.

In all of my sales roles I've been blown away by an overriding truth. Whenever I have put my attention on understanding what clients want, and had a really open conversation based on what they need and what they want to achieve, they nearly always go ahead with a purchase.

Having spent years secretly feeling very uncomfortable by being surrounded by those who had their prime focus on closing, I started to explore the possibility of opening in a more overt manner. At first my sales management teams were my guinea pigs but very quickly I couldn't help but notice the transformation in our sales results, our people and the whole energy of the environment shifted for the better when I put our attention on Opening.

I love selling and it is my heartfelt wish that you'll get to love it too, or love it even more than you already do.

Welcome to a magical world of sales.

Chapter One: L-O-V-E

The L-O-V-E Philosophy

'Eventually you will come to understand that love heals and love is all there is'

Gary Zukav

In every moment we have a choice. Shall we love or shall we fear?

Over the years I've worked closely with many, many sales people and also many non-sales people and the most profound thing that has stood out as a truth is this. When we choose fear, we constrict, we shrink, we panic, we under deliver, and we slide backwards into smaller and smaller versions of ourselves. We diminish, solutions become harder to find. Life becomes difficult and challenges appear insurmountable. We find our version of hell which is often dark, lonely and scary.

When we choose love, we choose a pathway that expands. People and places conspire to help and support us. We expand, we deliver, we include, we embrace, and we grow into the very best version of ourselves. We become brave, we over deliver, solutions pop up as if by magic, we soar; life is fulfilling and meaningful. We find our version of peace and joy.

Now before we get carried away with feeling the l-o-v-e, let me clarify.

In sales as in life:

- We still have to show up;

- We still have to do the work;

- We still require skills;

- We still have to participate.

We still have to choose, each and every day, between l-o-v-e and f-e-a-r. And sometimes that can be challenging as it can feel like that the choice is presenting itself in each and every moment of the day.

I'm not suggesting we ignore what frightens us. I'm not suggesting we bury our fears. There's an appropriate time to investigate our fears. There's an appropriate time to deal with fear. But right now, and in every single moment, we will create a far greater life for ourselves and others if we choose l-o-v-e. In fact, when the time does come to investigate our fears, even then, to do so having chosen l-o-v-e rather than f-e-a-r will smooth that process and we will heal so much quicker.

So how do we get started? And what does this have to do with selling?

The L-O-V-E philosophy outlines how you can start, or enhance, your successful life in sales. This four-step process will create and underpin a solid and robust foundation for a fulfilling, healthy, happy, profitable and enjoyable life in sales.

The four-steps of the L-O-V-E philosophy are

Step 1: Letting go – Releasing any preconceived notions of who you thought you ought to be, so that you can be the very best and authentic you.

Step 2: Opening – Creating in you the ability to be open to receive information without judgement, without prejudice and without outcome in mind.

Step 3: Value – To give and add value freely.

Step 4: Evaluation – Get those numbers down.

L-O-V-E: 'L'etting go – 'O'pening – 'V'alue – 'E'valuation

STEP 1: LETTING GO

What's letting go all about and why should we even consider letting go anyway? What are we likely to be letting go of, exactly? And what does this have to do with selling?

I have a question for you: Why do we sometimes insist on carrying the hefty burden of what's holding us back?

For some of us this can be a huge and obvious burden, for others perhaps one that we've known for years. We are scared, we don't want to be brave, and there are times when we definitely don't want to be a 'sales person'.

For many it is that subtle nagging feeling that we're just not good enough, clever enough, brave enough and can never be successful enough.

Why does it sometimes feel as though we've been carrying these burdens over millennia? We want them to go but they seem to linger, gnawing away at us. No matter how positive we are, no matter how many affirmations we chant at the mirror each morning, no matter how much time we meditate, do yoga, chase the bliss, they're still there.

Carrying the burden of who we think we should be, of what others think we should be and being who we think we ought to be can make us feel as though we're on the outside looking in. It's exhausting.

Why do we even get involved with the act of lugging around the insidious burden of fear; the fear of failing, fear of being too successful (oh yes my friends, sales people have that one too), and that pesky little fear – aka damned huge big mother of a fear – the fear of being fearful of not being in fear. Why on earth do we do that?

Excuse me? The fear… of being fearful… of not being in fear? Nearly lost you there – right?

Fear not!

Seriously though, why do we do this to ourselves? We could just let it go and travel forward with ease and poise. Purposefully march ahead without a single burden to weigh us down. And yet so often, or maybe only occasionally, we hold on to it. We tighten our grip even further and before we know it we're holding on for grim death. And when we do, it constricts and restricts us, it paralyses, it corrodes and damages us and it makes us smaller and smaller.

Why? Well, we're human – we do it.

You are not alone. You are not weird. It's not only you. We all do this some of the time and sometimes we do it all of the time; but the news is, we all do it.

So if we all do it, should we accept that we are we all doomed? No, definitely not.

So how do we start the process, or even accelerate the process, of letting go? And why would it benefit us to do so? How can we just *let go*?

There are many avenues that will take us there but in my experience first up is our state of awareness; being self-aware. Being aware of our go-to tendencies and then growing in awareness of how our personality traits feed us are good first steps to freeing ourselves and being able to commit to starting the process of letting go. The first baby step if you like. Over time, as our self-awareness develops, we tune in to ourselves in a more and more profound way. We soon start to realise that some of the values and beliefs we've been lugging around, some of our familiar go-to positions, have been creating restriction, causing constriction and serving us up a big old plate of playing small.

I believe that letting go is a process, a lifelong process, of adjustment, refinement, reflection and self-work. And it starts with our awareness of what's driving us and especially what we say to ourselves. Which internal voice we listen to the most and which internal dialogue is the narrative of our life.

Becoming aware of your self-talk; your internal dialogue. That voice; the one that barks instruction to you as you go about your day to day life. The one that's says, do this, don't do that, you need this, you don't need that. The one that says, 'Oh really, so you think you can do that do you?' The one that goes, 'Eewww' and turns its nose up at your dreams and what's important to you.

It tends to be harsh and unrelenting. It tends to be unforgiving, demanding, critical, and pushy and mean. It's that 'let's get you right where it hurts' kind of voice. It triggers you. It paralyses, it diminishes.

But it's the quiet voice, the one that quietly whispers, that is the true you. The gentle voice, the one that's soft, the one you initially really have to listen out for or you'll miss it. This is the powerful yet soft voice that nourishes, accepts and loves you, encourages, lifts you up, soothes and replenishes you; this is the voice of your true self. This is your voice of magnificence.

This is the voice that when you pay close attention to it will guide, direct and inspire you. It will lead you to a deep and profound understanding of who you are and how you can truly shine. I thoroughly recommend the book by La Rue Eppler and Vanessa Tabor Wesley called *Your Essential Whisper* which beautifully and elegantly describes how to get in touch with your whisper, in other words getting in touch with your true self.

In *Your Essential Whisper,* Eppler and Wesley talk about the values and beliefs that we pick up along the way and eventually interpret them as our own. The process Eppler has created is stellar in helping those of us who are committed to being our true selves and ultimately finding our truth. Their book helps us to start letting go of the noise.

We are hard wired to pick up values and beliefs from all sorts of innocent contributors as we journey along the road of life. I call them innocent contributors because we are mostly unaware of them as they quietly and powerfully contribute to our lives. We choose them. Then without realising it, we start to borrow and adopt the value and belief systems of these innocent contributors as we journey. At some point we wonder why we can't get true and meaningful satisfaction from our lives. We get frustrated at the drain down of our enthusiasm and the lack of motivation that inevitably ensues. As the puncture in our motivation slowly leaks, we tire, we become exhausted, and we fall prey to reaching out for whatever helps to numb the pain of life.

In the absence of living our own purposeful life, we can easily end up living out someone else's values and beliefs. It's not our dream; it's a half-baked dream of someone else. At worse, it's someone else's rule book as to how life should be lived. At best, it's our borrowed perception of what happiness is.

These innocent contributors have a massive impact on who we think we are and before long we create a menu of what we can and cannot do and who we should or should not be.

This adopted rule book, and let's stop for a moment to clarify; this is a rule book adopted by us. We consciously and unconsciously create it. However it very craftily works its way into what we believe happiness to be, it directs us to what happiness is supposed to feel like, what happiness sounds like and even what it looks like according to those innocent contributors.

Our innocent contributors come in many shapes and sizes – care givers, parents, colleagues, siblings, and media of all sorts. They are also our teachers, friends and co-workers. Anyone can be a contributor – after all, we get to choose, albeit that we are mostly choosing at an unconscious level so are blissfully unaware of the impact our choices are having on how we live our life.

Contributors can be resourceful or destructive. They can be helpful or they hinder you. They can build or crush. They may also have served a great purpose until now.

Letting go of who and what you think you should be… repeat… who and what you *think* you should be. Letting go of who and what you think others want you to be – repeat… who and what you *think* others want you to be – is a process that requires commitment.

It can be tough at times. Sometimes you may have to dig deep. Sometimes getting to the shift that makes the difference can seem perilously long and drawn out. But getting in touch with the very heart of who you are is a freeing, liberating, and a hugely expansive process. Reviewing all those values and beliefs you've adopted from contributors along the way is worth the occasional bumpy ride for a while. Deciding what you want to keep and what you want to let go is not always easy as you toss and turn in getting clear, but it's so worth it when you arrive at being you.

If it's right for you and you decide to commit to doing the work; dig deep, breathe into it and get really clear of who and what you are. Who and what you really want to be. You'll find you. The most amazing version, your true version will emerge and you'll be rewarded with energy, motivation, bravery and purpose and you'll expand in quantum leaps.

So what if you were to do this?

What if you were really prepared to do the work, dig deep and get really clear about exactly who you are and let go of any of the burdens that are stopping you being you?

I wonder what this may do for your sales results.

I wonder how this may translate into your business life, your sales life, your family life, social life and all of the other areas of life.

It's time for us to be whole; live life with a 360° view.

I have long been wary of those who say their business life is totally separate to their personal life. I kind of want to say, 'Really?' You know the ones who say, 'Well, it's business isn't it?' which, oddly enough, tends to follow shortly after a particularly cruel and devastating blow has been launched.

So, who you are in your business life is so separate to that of your personal life that I won't recognise you? What's okay for you to do in your business life wouldn't happen in your private life? Really?

So what you're really saying is that you show up differently in your different lives?

Sure, we may have different priorities in the various areas of our lives, but showing up differently in business than in personal lives? Showing up differently in our sales life than in our family life? Not on my watch, baby, not for me. Not anymore. I am who I am.

Let's just be who we are. Be who you are. We can add some skills along the way; we can always learn a new technique or two, or a hundred for that matter. We can take a class, research, surf the net, check out the latest Ted Talks, but please, for the love of all things true, just start by just letting go and be you. Not a version of you but the real you.

STEP 2: OPENING

In the majority of sales literature, sales chit chat and most things to do with sales, the conversation nearly always turns to 'closing the sale'. This pre-occupation with 'closing' has always troubled me. I'm bored and unimpressed with 'closing' being the go-to topic of sales, and have been for years. I'm over the one-upmanship, the noise, the trickery, the perceived manipulation, the nonsense of so called closing.

Question time:

If our main focus is about 'closing' who are we thinking about?

How successful are we in sales when the main focus is about us 'closing the sale'?

And by sales success I mean a full bodied, totally rounded, ecological, profitable, fulfilling and sustainable kind of success. Not the grab it and run version.

The energy around the preoccupation of the 'closing rules' brigade repels me. It feels off, it feels ego driven, it feels stale and 'so last century, darling'. It feels yuk and in my experience it delivers yuk too.

Of course it is important at some point to draw the sales conversation to a conclusion, wrap up the meeting, and bring closure to a particular transaction. But that's not what I'm talking about here. I'm talking about the preoccupation with closing the deal that populates a lot of sales literature and sales conversations, doing whatever it takes to get the deal, closing down the client using whatever tactics can be mustered.

I have a few more questions for you.

I wonder what it would be like if you spend the time you have, and the valuable time of your clients, by concentrating on opening?

I wonder what would happen if your focus was all about 'opening'?

If you think about opening who are you thinking about?

How successful could we all be if the main focus was about opening, and about being open?

If you're up for letting go of what feels bad and doesn't serve you anymore – you are primed to opening up to what is great. Right at the heart of successful selling is the ability and willingness to be open. Not only is it easier, it's far more pleasurable and it actually delivers superior results.

As you open up to the best version of yourselves you also open up to your full potential and in doing so, the many opportunities available to you and your clients. Having an authentic connection with your clients, being open and staying open, is a sure pathway to serving with grace.

Serving with grace is the cornerstone of successful, profitable and ecological sales.

Embrace this and when you do, it is always one of those moments that shifts us, takes us to a new level of understanding, a new paradigm. Can we LOVE SELLING? Can we learn how to sell without selling out?

Oh yes we can baby. Let's do this – but how?

- You will need some skills – in particular, some communication skills will be useful. The good news is that you've been using many of these skills all of your life, so at some level you'll know them, but I'll put them together in the most powerful and useful fashion for you. We're going to do that together later on in the book.

- You're going to want a sales process so that the time you spend with your clients is productive and efficient. We're going to do that too.

- You're going to want some information on how to prepare. That's covered.

- I know you'll benefit from jumping into some detail about how we tick, that's you, me and our clients.

- It'll almost certainly help you if you knew a little about what makes us want to move towards buying something. Please note: that'll be about your client buying something and not you flogging something. That's all covered too.

- I'll cover the before, during, and after sales stuff so you'll be completely clear about what's helpful for you and your clients, when it's helpful, and why.

- And there's a whole bunch more stuff too which will include things like presenting your solution, connection and generally having a blast whilst building your sales. Oh sorry, I forgot to mention, you can enjoy this. In fact, I've found it really helps if you do.

I've got this. So for now, let's get really clear about the power of opening ourselves.

How do we open ourselves? And once open, how do we maintain that connection with ourselves so that we can connect with our clients?

First up, there is a prerequisite, which is that we actually care.

If you do not care then this is not for you. I'm serious. If you do not care about your clients or about yourself for that matter, then close this book right now and move on. In fact, if you only care about yourself then please move on too. Please leave. Nice knowing you briefly and this is not for you. Adios amigos – have a great life and please let it be somewhere else.

If you do care, I mean really care, this is likely to be the start of the shift in your sales life.

Opening ourselves:

Being open and staying open is a toughie.

No matter how enlightened you may be, how awake you consider yourself, how evolved, no matter how practised or experienced you are in sales, or no matter how little experience you have in sales, the act of being open and staying open is one that will require continual development, self-monitoring and adjustment.

In the context of the sales arena; communicating with a client, truly caring and staying open is a behaviour that most of us humans have a fair way to go before we achieve mastery. You will probably have work to do. I do. It requires continual adjustment, continual checking-in that you are still on point. Having the discipline to frequently check-in that you are open is the best and most effective pathway to serving a client.

So what do I actually mean by being open and staying open – and why is it so important?

Being open, truly open, is to create within you, in any particular moment, an empty vessel in order to receive. Receive without judgement, without prejudice, without outcome in mind. To be available to the information that is in front of you, to actively listen and to take on board the energy and the needs of another in a given situation. To be fully present in that moment. To suspend your unrelated thoughts, concerns and worries. To focus without interruption on what is required within a particular situation.

This is a mindful act of deliberately suspending the 'me' and the 'I' so that you can concentrate on the needs of your client. We will cover client needs later, but for now, let's just accept that the client may or may not be fully aware of all their needs. So, being open is an absolutely critical state for you to be in, such that you can meet the client where they are at. Walk in their shoes and discover with them what's important; what they need and want. Being open is at the heart of any good quality engagement. It's at the heart of all great communication; the platform that supports you being able to actively listen to your client. It's where serving with grace starts.

Being in a state of openness requires discipline, it has the prerequisite that you genuinely care for your clients and are dedicated to the concept that the best outcome is the one that serves the highest good of all.

This will mean that sometimes you will not have the right product or service for your client. That's fine. Sometimes the outcome will be a no-sale. That's fine too. What you will always leave with is your integrity and your client will be whole. It starts with being open and develops by remaining, and then maintaining, that openness.

It starts with you.

Opening clients:

Opening your clients is the most effective way in which you can serve them. If you are not interested in what a client really wants and needs, what's important to them, how can you serve appropriately? Holding the space for your client such that opening occurs with ease and elegance is the most important element of a sale. It is the single most effective way to ensure that your client's needs are met.

I'll be covering some specific communication skills later on which will support you and help you understand what your client needs and wants, so that it'll be easy to figure out if you have a solution to help them.

You are a problem solver – that's what being in sales is all about. Good quality sales are about solving your client's problems with the products and services in your portfolio. You may not be able to help everyone but you'll never know unless you really understand what your client needs and wants. What's truly important to them?

Approaching sales with the intention of being open and establishing your clients' needs will ensure that you serve with passion, deliver a world class service and enjoy exemplary customer satisfaction. You will definitely create more sales. Your sales success will be a direct line to that of your openness. It will correlate with precision as to how much you understood the needs of your client.

It all starts with being open and caring about meeting the needs of your client.

I'll cover exactly how we do this later in the S-E-L-L-I-N-G chapters but for now, I wonder if you can imagine what would happen if your client meetings always started by being open and opening up to your client's needs.

What if you were able to deliver what your client needed, in a package that really works for you both? I wonder how good that will feel. What will your clients say about you? How many referrals will you have? What will your sales results look like?

STEP 3: VALUE

Step 3 of the L-O-V-E philosophy is all about Value.

What value do you add? Why is it important to add value? In fact, let's back up a little. What value do you bring to the party?

Value: The regard that something is held to deserve; the importance, worth, or usefulness of something… The worth of something compared to the price paid or asked for it.

The Oxford Dictionary

In a world that's cluttered with information and competing noise, over-stimulated with numerous media sources, data streaming from all directions, cascades of information available at a key stroke – what value do you bring? What precise value do you bring to your client?

Make sure you are as up to date as possible with what's going on in your market place; the current environment, how the landscape is changing, evolving or shifting in your sector. Be aware of what competitors may offer. Know if there are any imitators in your sector. Ensure you understand the benefits of your products and services; why they are great and very importantly, what problems do they solve and who are they likely to help?

In other words, what do you know and what can you bring to the party?

Like the other three steps in the L-O-V-E philosophy it's a continual learning process. It's continually re-visiting what you know and updating your knowledge accordingly. It's being committed to continually upgrading your learning. It's an on-going process of self-development. It never ends.

How do you do it?

- You are always alert for new information that will grow your knowledge; anything that develops your understanding of your products and services.

- You are clear on why your products and services are great – you know what problems they solve.

- You deepen your understanding of your client and what they want to achieve, what they need, what's important to them.

- You make it your business to understand the challenges your client may be facing and the time lines that may be of importance to them.

- You read websites – cover to cover. Especially your own.

- You network within your industry.

- You network outside your industry.

- You connect with suppliers; you become friends with the manufacturers' representatives.

- You have an inbuilt curiosity to everything and anything that relates to your market place, your clients, your environment and your business.

- You immerse yourself in what you do.

So when the time comes to meet with your client, you add value. You add proper value that exceeds anything that they may be likely to buy from you. You set a clear protocol for yourself that your value will always exceed the monetary tag. Always.

- If your product or service is £1,000, you deliver a minimum of £1,001 value – or greater.

- If the widget you recommend as a solution is $4, you deliver a minimum of $4.01 value – or greater.

- If your treatment solution is €99; a minimum of €100 value must be delivered – or greater.

Your clients will quickly come to know and appreciate what you bring to the party and you'll become the support they want and need. In no time you'll be the reliable source of excellence they turn to in order to solve their problems.

Your job as a sales person is to help solve your client's problems.

Whenever you possibly can, always add more value than anyone was expecting. It will deepen your existing client relationships and promote recommendations, referrals and testimonials. And even beyond the fact that the value that you add oils your client relationships immeasurably, it also feels great.

Feeling great, well, it just feels great. Remember, you are allowed to enjoy yourself and feel great. It's all part of the LOVE SELLING experience.

STEP 4: EVALUATION

Evaluation is a crucial step yet it can often be ignored, which we do at our peril. Evaluation is all about the numbers.

In order to steer your ship, you absolutely have a need to be aware of your numbers.

The metrics of your individual sales performance and globally across the business are critical. Please note: this is *your* business so the numbers are definitely your responsibility.

Regardless of the industry or the environment, or if you work for a global corporate or a small local firm, or if you're a sole trader or freelancer, or if you work for someone or are self-employed, one thing is for sure – if you are not aware of the metrics of your individual performance and those of your immediate business it will be akin to trying to steer a rudderless boat. Very quickly you will be confused, demotivated and could possibly create problems for yourself.

So what do I mean by evaluation and why bother?

Evaluating your performance on an individual and global level is critical to know how you're doing. Failure to do this will create a breeding ground for mediocrity. You will have no way of identifying real issues, no plan for systematic sales improvement and you will almost certainly drift. You will lose focus and you will put your success in jeopardy.

If you do not pay attention to the metrics of your business, or that of your sales performance, apart from the fact that you will have no idea how you're doing, you will also have no idea how to improve in a systematic fashion.

Numbers are the guideposts for any business and especially in sales.

It's not difficult and you don't have to be a qualified accountant. You don't have to be incredibly numerate but you do need to ensure that this element of your sales life is taken care of – by you.

Being guided by the leadership team, if appropriate, or compiling your own dashboard that accurately reflects the mechanics of your business will give you immediate and clear insight. You'll have access when and if something goes wrong or isn't working the way you intended and you'll be in a far better position to react in a calm and thoughtful manner as to how you can self-correct and be even more successful.

Metrics are not a nice to have, they are not a luxury – they are an imperative. They will act as guideposts for adjustments and growth that could deliver superb outcomes financially.

It's your performance and it's your business. Even if you work for someone else, it's still your performance within their business. Getting clear on what the key numbers are, the key metrics which will drive the business towards success is a great starting point for devising a dashboard that will support you throughout each week, month, quarter and ultimately the financial year.

It requires a little thought and effort, but once done and updated regularly it will give you clarity and certainty in your business management. It's really quite relaxing knowing that you're unlikely to have a nasty surprise and can concentrate on delivering excellence instead. Of course another benefit is that you'll have a solid platform to work from when you start the planning process for your next year.

So let's get the numbers down, sort them out straight away, and get clear on what the metrics are that will drive your business or what metrics are important to your sales performance, so that you can get on with delivering value to the business. What data may be useful for marketing purposes now and in the future? What sales metrics ensure that the business thrives? If you don't know these, find out what they are and get them down. Include them in your personal dashboard so that you have a robust platform from which to work.

Get clear on what's important to record; document it, then update and review frequently. Do this early on and you'll have created a template for your own self-improvement and your sales performance and the business will have a chance of thriving.

Let's take a closer look at what these numbers may look like.

Taking the macro view, you'll want to know what's coming into your business in terms of client enquiries or sales leads and, ultimately, what's converting into a sale and what is not. In its most basic form, what is your overall sales conversion?

In other words, what and how many sales have been achieved from the leads or enquiries you've had?

Are your sales leads in the form of phone contacts made, visits made, or maybe both? Perhaps they take the form of visitors into your store, clinic, or outlet. Do they start out as enquiries via your website, your social media, walk-ins or recommendations from previous clients? Whatever their original form, record their entry into your business and start documenting your sales progress from that point.

You'll know how many enquiries you have coming into your business, but where are they and where did they come from?

This is not only interesting from your point of view but will also really help those who are responsible for the marketing. And if you're responsible for your own marketing this will definitely assist you in creating a more successful and refined marketing plan that generates even more enquiries, sales leads, customers and clients.

It's really straightforward and easy to do but it's important to be consistent in your monitoring. Wherever the starting point is for an enquiry to enter the sales function, start there. Capture everything that may be important to you or your marketing team and then proceed by getting into the detail about the journey and lifetime of that lead.

To be really clear, a lifetime of any enquiry and any sales lead is forever!

It either converts into a sale now, sometime in the near future, or sometime in the distant future, but it is never a waste of time and it is never ever to be disgarded. For the inexperienced, and actually sometimes for those who think they're very experienced, discarding enquiries and sales leads is a mistake that is frequently made.

Discarding a lead at any point during the customer journey is not only wasteful but also commercially foolish. Even if the prospect never buys your product they may be an advocate of the products and services you offer and recommend you to friends, family and co-workers. If you make it your business to treat everyone with the same level of positive energy at the enquiry stage you'll soon gain a reputation for being a pleasure to engage with, and sales will follow.

I have had the benefit of working with teams who were extremely lead poor but were sales rich because they treated every single lead as though it were gold dust. Without exception, they took every previous lead and recognised that there was a human being on the other end of the enquiry sheet. That kind of respect travels well. Unsurprisingly, time and time again, those are the teams and sales people who enjoy the greatest success in their sales conversions.

Once a sale is achieved there are a gazillion other metrics that come into play. It may be volume of sales, revenue, product split, payment type, promotions or campaign-led sales. The list is endless so it should be a matter that you consider carefully so as not to get tangled up in endless reporting.

But it's also in the robust analysis of why an enquiry or sales lead didn't sell, that great riches lie. That's where you'll learn about elements that you missed, you'll get feedback on prodcuts and services and find out what you could have done to better serve your client. Spending quality time on evaluating the no sales is just as powerful as reviewing what did sell. It'll give you room for growth and you'll be able to more accurately modify the time with your next client.

Every number in sales has a value that far exceeds its face value. So getting really comfortable with your metrics will guide you so that you can grow your sales and business.

It really is straightforward.

What do you want to achieve? Where are your sales leads or customers coming from and in what way do they show up? What are the client touch points as the lead jouneys towards either becoming a sale or a no sale? When a sale is achieved – what happens to ensure customer satisfaction? What happens to that enquiry when a sale hasn't yet been achieved?

In a nutshell, you really want to know absolutely every posisble aspect of the outcome of an initial enquiry and nurture it to ensure a superior customer experience.

Make this part of your daily, weekly and monthly routine and you'll be well on your way to having a thorough understanding of what's going on in your sales performance and in your business.

It's down to you to take the action.

THE L.O.V.E. PHILOSOPHY

LETTING GO

OPEN HEARTED

OPENING

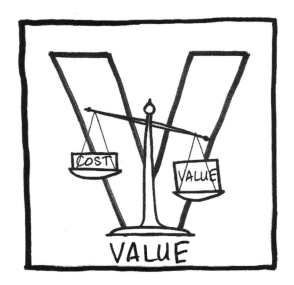

COST

VALUE

VALUE

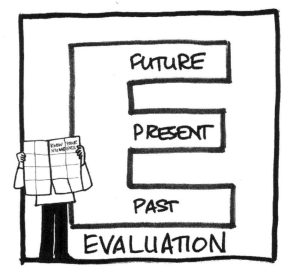

FUTURE

PRESENT

PAST

EVALUATION

What are the key principles of the L-O-V-E philosophy?

The L-O-V-E philosophy is specifically designed to create the necessary space so that you can dive into your sales with passion, vitality and purpose.

Letting Go – Releasing any pre-conceived notions of who you thought you ought to be so that you can be the very best and authentic You.

Opening – To create in you the ability to be open to receive information without judgement, without prejudice and without outcome in mind.

Value – To give and add value freely.

Evaluation – Get those numbers down.

The four pillars will support and serve you so that you can support and serve others.

It's an ongoing development of self that is at the heart of being ready and prepared to serve with poise when you meet your client. You'll be clear, focused and ready and they will sense the openness and clearly know the value you bring.

L-O-V-E S-E-L-L-I-N-G

With the energy of love in your heart, and the four-step L-O-V-E Philosophy as your foundation let's make the dive into selling.

The S-E-L-L-I-N-G process is a formula designed to give you what you need in order to grow your sales tool box. S-E-L-L-I-N-G gives you the tools, techniques and skill set to dramatically enhance your existing successful sales career. Or for those of you starting out in sales it will give you everything you need to know to get started.

Personal growth in sales is never ending – to achieve mastery is an on-going process which just when you think you've got there, you realise that there's so much more to learn and so much more to discover. There's a great deal of joy in amongst it all. It's a continuous process looping back and forth between working on a particular element of your sales process, nailing it and then revisiting and reviewing how it's serving your clients and your business, and then perhaps going away to work on it a little more.

It's just fantastic.

I love SELLING and I want to show you how to LOVE SELLING too. For me there's an even greater component to LOVE SELLING; and that's, how to sell without selling out.

So how do you grow your sales ecologically? How do you sell with integrity? How do you build your sales performance and keep everyone and everything whole? How do you maintain openness whilst wanting to conclude the business?

How can you LOVE SELLING, without selling out?

For me it's been a long and wonderful romance. It's been tough at times and ridiculously easy at others. It's been hugely rewarding and sometimes challenging, sometimes gentle and at other times explosive with passion, and I've loved it all.

It's been about falling in love with the idea of how fun it is to serve another, the joyful energy that radiates from us when we truly connect with another human being. Above all, selling and being in sales is great fun and deeply satisfying.

It is my intention that you get the most from your sales in an authentic, powerful and congruent way so that you and your clients are served with grace. That you and your clients remain whole and the highest good is achieved for all parties.

So how do you sell without selling out?

I promised some skills, I promised a little bit of science, and I promised some process and structure.

So let's do this.

The S-E-L-L-I-N-G process covers everything you'll need to know to be your very best version and totally awesome in sales. If you're prepared to put some work in, it'll be easy and straightforward. The more you put in, the more you practice, you'll find the easier it'll become, and the more you and your clients will enjoy the sales experience.

So what's it all about? Let's run through what we'll be diving into.

Introduction to the S-E-L-L-I-N-G Process

'S'-E-L-L-I-N-G

The **'S'** is about **SETTING INTENTIONS.**

This is about setting intentions for yourself and also for your client.

Understanding the power of setting intentions will change your world. It has mine, and I can't wait to share with you how really easy it is to do. Once you get your focus exactly how you want it in your life and in your sales world, you'll manifest beyond your wildest dreams. It's magical.

S-'E'–L-L-I-N-G

The **'E'** is about **ENTERING THE SALE.**

This is all about the preparation that's required in order to deliver excellence.

Your preparations before you enter a sales visit or sales call.

It's making sure that you have everything you need in order to shine and be your best version when you're with your client. It covers who can help you, how you can help yourself and where to find the natural resources which are available to support and strengthen you and your proposition.

S-E-'L'-L-I-N-G

The first **'L'** is all about **LEARNING.**

Learning about your client so that you can serve them properly.

It's about asking good quality questions that lead to good quality conversations that are always productive and efficient and make sense to your client. It's the key to finding out what your client needs, what they want and what's important to them.

S-E-L-'L'-I-N-G

This **'L'** is about **LISTENING.**

Tuning into yourselves and your clients and listening with your heart.

There are two elements to listening in this section.

Warning: This is no ordinary listening. The first kind of listening is about listening to yourself. It's about learning to hear the whisper of your soul, tapping into who you really are and really long to be. It's listening to the yearning of your soul and choosing to act upon it. It's a beautiful process of honouring yourself in this moment which leads to powerful transformation. It's stunningly sublime.

The second kind of listening is that of listening to your clients; listening in a profound and deep way so that they are truly heard. A gift that business is yearning for across our planet.

S-E-L-L-'I'-N-G

Next up is **'I'** which is for **INVOLVE**.

The energy of connection and collaboration.

How can you ensure your clients are actively involved and included in the sales process? How can you ensure it's a collaborative process and not just something that you 'do' to them?

We'll be jumping into the science of motivation, taking a peek into rapport and connection and generally investigating ways that your clients will know that you're truly interested in them. Your clients will be involved, and feel involved, throughout the sales process.

S-E-L-L-I-'N'-G

'N' is about **NEEDS.**

Establishing what your client needs is central to understanding what they want and what's important to them.

Get this piece right and you'll be able to offer relevant and appropriate solutions. Get this bit wrong and you'll be like any other unsuccessful sales person desperately trying to flog stuff.

Establishing needs is a biggie so I'm going to dive into some of the science behind needs, how they get born and developed, and a whole bunch of other useful information that will help you to truly deliver excellence for your clients.

S-E-L-L-I-N-'G'

'G' is GENUINE YES.

Genuine Yes is about presenting a solution based on your client's unique and specific needs. It's about serving. It's about creating a safe and appropriate reason for a client to want to buy. It's not about flogging stuff.

We are going to talk about money, how to present the price and how to bring the sales conversation to a natural conclusion.

Very importantly we're also going to talk about following up on no sales. Not only how this is inextricably linked to higher sales conversions but also to increased client satisfaction, referrals, recommendation and such like.

Once the full L-O-V-E S-E-L-L-I-N-G experience has been covered I'll bring it all together in a wrap-up and we'll review the flow of the whole philosophy and process.

When L-O-V-E and S-E-L-L-I-N-G are synthesised the true experience of serving with grace and deep joy purposefully emerges.

Ready? Well, let's do this then!

Chapter 2: SELLING – SETTING INTENTIONS

Setting intentions for yourself and also for your client

*'The only way to get what you really want is to know
what you really want.
The only way to know what you really want is to know yourself.
The only way to know yourself is to be yourself.
And the only way to be yourself is to listen to your heart.'*

Mike Dooley – Messages from the Universe

There's a universal law to setting intentions: 'Once an intention is set with conviction, the Universe and everything in it conspires to help us achieve it.' Paulo Coelho said that and it's certainly a universal truth.

It was at the back end of 1999, towards the end of November, and I was a Regional Sales Manager for a large corporate in the UK. My Region produced just over £50m of sales turnover per annum. Around about this time each year we were issued with our sales targets for the forthcoming year. Our financial year started on 1st January and typically a few weeks beforehand the Head of Sales would bring the senior management team together and issue these targets.

I turned up to the meeting confident but exhausted. My team and I had had a good year but it would be these final weeks of the year that would make all the difference. The seasonality of our business was such that the last couple of months would be the busiest. They would, without a shadow of doubt, prove to be the difference between a successful year and an awesome year. It was worth working six days a week during these couple of months but even on the seventh day my mind was buzzing with the thought of what else could be done to get us significantly over the line. End the year on a high – over deliver on our annual target.

Tracking down every single sale, following up every single customer that was still to decide, ensuring that every one of my sales managers was coping with the additional pressure, keeping everyone engaged and making sure that every single sales person across the region was connected with what was needed to be done.

The Head of Sales meeting was underway – it was time for the target reveal. The science of how the targets had been calculated had been explained. We were painstakingly taken through the mathematics, the rationale behind the national target, and the calculations of how this had been split between the three regions. It all made sense, it was all absolutely rational, totally fair, the science made complete business sense. And then the reveal itself; £ x million to the northern region, £ x to the central region and £75,000,000 to me. I could do all but hold my breath and pretend I was ok. It was a massive target. Way, way higher than the previous year. Way higher than the other two regions. Way, way higher than I had anticipated.

I won't lie; as soon as I got in my car to drive home that evening I started to cry. I cried and cried all the way home. By the time I eventually reached home, some three hours later, I was exhausted but in a different way to how I had arrived that morning. I felt absolutely depleted, totally spent. I doubted that I could cry any more although I was soon to find out that I could. The whole evening at home was a blur, interspersed with feelings of utter exhaustion and then crying some more. Although I knew I really had to pull myself together and start planning how I would reveal the news to my management team; I fell into bed, pulled the duvet over my head and tried to sleep.

What I failed to mention is that with this target went a pay plan; my pay plan and that of my managers. Our pay plans were inextricably linked to the over-achievement of target. In that moment of the target reveal, I had potentially witnessed my income for the following year, and that of my management team, flush itself straight down the toilet.

After a very patchy and disturbed sleep, I woke up slightly glassy eyed, slightly hung-over from crying and it was then that I made a decision.

This was going to be my best year ever.

In that moment, as crazy as it sounded; I decided that this was going to be my best year ever. I mean *ever*.

I'm still not entirely sure if this was a polar reaction to me feeling immense fear, or if it was due to some kind of divine intervention but one thing was for sure; I was going to have a good year and in fact a great year at that. I owed it to myself and to my team.

If I'm perfectly honest, at this stage it really was about me and what I wanted. I wanted a good year. I wanted to overachieve and I wanted to earn as much as I had in previous years. I wanted this so much I could feel energy starting to flow into my veins. In that moment I had absolutely no idea how, but I knew one thing for sure: I was going to achieve it!

In that moment I set the intention for my best year ever. I decided that I was going to over achieve – regardless of how I felt in that moment.

Now let's be clear. It wasn't going to happen simply because I thought how nice it would be. I knew only too well what was ahead of me. The success of the Region was hugely complex. I had seven direct report managers, who each had around twenty direct reports. Then there were the internal departments, with which I needed to work very closely – they had been issued entirely different targets, which were not aligned to mine. There was just a whole bunch of stuff that could go wrong and, what made it worse, was that the control was not only with me. Even if I had been a totally amazing specimen of a Regional Sales Manager, it wasn't going to be just down to me. There were massive external factors poised to screw this up. I might add that this was much to my irritation as I am a self-confessed control freak. It's something I'm still working on… well, sort of, kind of, periodically, still working on.

But what I did have in place was an amazing management team who I trusted implicitly. We had worked together for two to three years at this stage and I regarded them highly. They were dedicated, honest and powerful in their resolve. They were talented. I had a hugely committed sales force. They knew what they were doing, they accepted training and coaching continually and they were open to being connected to this larger regional team that my managers and I had created.

I quickly revealed the new targets to my management team and shared what I wanted to achieve. I gave direction to how I thought this may pan out, what we may have to do, how deep we may have to dig and we spent a couple of days pulling our strategy together for the following year.

Over the months that followed, nothing – and I mean nothing – would prevent me from seeking out, finding new ways, exploring and reviewing old ways and searching for any opportunity that would get me over that line of £75,000,000. My management team had chosen to mirror my desire of over-achievement. No stone was left unturned. We were on fire.

Although I was challenged continually throughout the year, no matter what happened, my focus was on doing the work that would deliver the intention I had set myself just before the previous Christmas holidays.

The following year the numbers came in and the overachievement was secure. My team and I had delivered in a most spectacular fashion. It was the highest regional sales achievement ever within the organisation and arguably one the organisation may not have really envisaged me achieving. My team and I celebrated, we hugged, we actually cried. Well, I cried. But it was when I went home on the day of our celebration, exhausted but happy beyond words, that I realised that it had all started when I set the intention some fourteen months beforehand.

At the time of setting my intention, I was no more skilled than my fellow regional colleagues, no more talented, no more gifted and no luckier. But I was clear in my intention. Very, very clear. Crystal clear, in fact. I wanted it so badly that it became part of my DNA. In that moment, it was what I really, really wanted. I set my intention and then concentrated on doing the work required to deliver it. Relentlessly.

Apart from having the glow of over-achievement, apart from the joy that my team had delivered when it really counted, apart from all the team stuff which has always been so important to me, I also ended up earning more that year than I ever previously dreamt possible. I had become the highest earning individual within the history of our regional sales management team by a significant measure, and in fact had apparently also earned more than many of the directors within the organisation. Now that's a story for another time. But even more important than all of this, that one year not only set me up financially, it also set me up in a fulfilling and happy career that followed. I gained a reputation within the industry as being a force to be reckoned with, an over-achiever, and the person who would deliver. It gave me confidence that I wouldn't otherwise have had, an opportunity that I had never imagined possible, and it led to a business and a lifestyle that I adore.

All because I set a very clear intention and then put my heart and soul into doing the work to deliver it.

Intentions are powerful phenomena. They plug into the law of the universe; its cause and effect. You put it out there, you take serious action and *boom* you get spectacular results.

For me, there's something exquisite about setting an intention rather than just setting a goal. Although goals are important too, setting an intention seems so much more expansive, so huge, so much bigger than ourselves, so much more than we would normally consider we could achieve. It's magical. There just seems to be so much more scope. Setting intentions gives me courage, makes me brave, allows me to dream beyond my education, beyond my geographical location, beyond who I am today. When I set my intentions I grow and stretch myself.

I set intentions for large and small things – in fact, for mostly everything these days. I set the intention for how I'd like the client meeting to go, how I want a call to go, the direction of my business, my relationships, friendships, my leisure time, family time. I set intentions for it all.

Sometimes, life gets in the way and I forget. That's often when the outcomes aren't quite how I had imagined them, not purposeful and fulfilling. I sometimes short-change myself.

It's an ongoing process of deliberate intention-setting that catapults us forward.

Set the intention, get it really clear so that you can then get on with the work required to deliver it.

So what do you really want? I mean, *really* want?

Take the time out to 'have a meeting with yourself' – oh by the way, I thoroughly recommend having meetings with yourself. They are super productive.

The rules of a 'Meeting with Yourself' are:

- Attendees 1
- Agenda
  - what do I want to discuss with myself today?
  - what outcomes do I want on a particular topic?
- Phone (or phones) off, laptop shut down, all devices switched off.
- Coffee

Seriously, when you have a meeting with yourself, life becomes so much clearer. You create space between you and everything that's going on around you. You get perspective.

The three layers of Intention Setting:

So how can you set intentions that are meaningful to you and will serve your pathway?

I've found that there are three main layers of Intention Setting.

Layer 1: Global

Layer 2: Time bound

Layer 3: In the moment

Layer 1: Global

What do you want for you? Taking a global, high level, big chunk view of your life, what do you want?

In what direction would you most like your life to go?

Setting global intentions, sets the overall direction of your future. Getting a directional perspective on what it is that you want and where it may be.

As your intentions in this layer are those which determine your direction, they act as your signposts to creating and living your life the way you find most fulfilling. A bit like if you were creating a feature length movie of your life – what genre movie do you want to create?

Take a look over the seven key areas of your life. One of my teachers and influencers, Dr John Demartini, advocates that what you value, or what's important to you, is where your passion is likely to reside. You may wish to start by choosing two or three from these seven areas. He states that these will likely be the areas of your life that hold the most value and interest for you. The areas of your life you most enjoy are the ones you'll most naturally choose and are likely to provide the most fulfilment and joy.

Vocational – your work

Financial – your money

Physical – your body

Family – your family and extended family

Spiritually – your relationship with the divine

Social – your friends and activities

Mental – your mind

Setting intentions for all of these areas at once may be overwhelming, but choosing two or three areas and taking the time out to get really clear will serve in getting you what you most desire out of this thing called life.

Getting your direction clear and by that I mean the big picture of where you are going, will help you in all sorts of ways.

It will support your time management skills. Knowing if something aligns with what you want in your life makes the decision so much easier to make when faced with the endless distractions that pass by. You'll definitely know what to choose and what to let go of, if you've set a clear intention for your path.

It helps with saying yes or no to well-meaning folk, business opportunities or invitations of any kind. It either aligns with your intention or it doesn't. The choice becomes very easy and freeing.

It helps with stamina. Setting clear intentions will also boost your energy. The global intention by nature gives way to a plan. Once you have a plan; even if you don't yet have the precise details of how to achieve your plan, you will have a direction. This direction alone gives you the internal fuel, which boosts you to take the first step towards eventual lift-off. It separates what supports you and what pulls you down. It makes energy sappers drift away. It makes it much more challenging for energy sappers to draw you into situations, activities and topics that don't align with your intention. They'll still be there, they'll still try to sap your energy, but the difference is you'll be able to quickly and easily differentiate between what fuels you and what drains you. Eventually it'll become your reliable internal satellite navigation.

Layer 2: Time Bound

These are the intentions that have particular value to you within a specific time frame. That annual target, the weekly sales target, gaining and absorbing knowledge. If you like, these are a particularly important scene in your feature length movie.

You may wish to take two areas from your global intentions and work them harder within the time-frame section. Break them open and start to put your plan together with some meaningful time frames around what's important to you.

The same rules apply, it's just that you're now getting more and more specific within the time-bound intention setting exercise. Get really specific.

Your time management will become stellar. It either fits with what you're going for or not. Your decisions become easier and easier. And because you're getting clearer and clearer, your energy seems to jump up a notch.

Layer 3: In the moment

Lastly, and just as important as the other two layers, are setting intentions in the moment. These are the individual frame shots, a frame within a scene, within your feature length movie.

Your client meeting, your sales call, being open, staying open, letting go; these can also take the form of an affirmation which many people find hugely supportive.

The more and more you develop your intention setting muscle, the stronger your muscle becomes. You're presented with a situation. In that moment, get clear on what you want, set your intention and move on to doing whatever needs to be done to deliver it.

As your intention muscle gets stronger and stronger, it will become second nature to be really specific and really clear. Clarity gives you certainty which boosts your clarity of purpose. It propels you forward with precision like purpose. Your energy will be clear, you will find it easier and easier to align with what it is you really want, and you will manifest at a greater speed for yourself and others.

So what do you really want?

Layer 1: Globally

Layer 2: Time bound

Layer 3: In the moment

Let's make a list.

What kind of sales life do you want? Set the intention.

Who are your ideal clients? Set the intention.

How do you want to work? Set the intention.

What do you want to achieve? Set the intention.

When do you want to achieve it? Set the intention.

How do you want to be paid? Set the intention.

When do you want to get paid? Set the intention

Where do you want to work? Set the intention.

You get to decide who, what and how you'll be. It's down to you. You'll serve yourself and others exquisitely if you do.

My NLP (Neuro Linguistic Programming) teacher and mentor was and is an amazing lady called Dr Susi Strang. After years in the British National Health Service as a General Practitioner she became a teacher of NLP, where she could apply her love of learning and teaching. She was, and is, formidable.

She built a clinic and training facility alongside her home in North Yorkshire, UK, where she practiced as a psychotherapist and taught NLP amongst other subjects.

During the two years of studying under her tutorship I was always stunned as to how she delivered her work. An academic through and through she also had the warmth of a thousand angels. I adored learning with her.

But there was even more to this learning experience than the academic curriculum. Throughout the two-year period, every time I made the eight-hour journey to my classes, she never failed to serve the most delicious home-cooked soup and a gorgeous selection of bread. She made the soup herself. Every day was a new recipe, different flavours, and different textures; every day she made us, her students, home-made soup. As a self-confessed foodie, I loved our lunches.

One day in particular stands out for me though, even now after all these years. It was 12th September 2001, the day after the world was struck by the horror of 9/11. I had sat up all night with my friend Caron Waddington, with whom I was lodging, watching TV and transfixed by the news that was pouring out of New York. Bleary eyed and still in shock like the rest of the world, we turned up at class the following day. After a soulful morning of discussions about what had happened in New York we started our NLP lessons. When we broke for lunch there was, as always, Susi's home-made soup. I couldn't believe that amongst everything else that was going on in the world, Susi had still made sure we were provided for by serving her own home-made soup.

I found out much later that when Susi first started her private practice, she had set the intention that all her students would feel nourished and looked after under her tutelage. One of the ways she delivered that intention was to make home-made soup for lunch each day. Dr Susi Strang's intention to nourish us and look after us worked. I certainly felt cared for and I'm sure I'm not her only student who remembers this. I'm sure we all have taken our version of it forward into our work today.

So what is it that you intend for your clients? What intentions are you willing to set for your client such that they benefit?

Is it that you're willing to set the intention that you'll stay open to their needs?

That you'll do whatever it takes to deliver excellence?

That your client will feel comfortable with the meeting?

Will your intention for your client be to hold the space so that they are able to feel free to discuss what it is that they really want and need?

Do you intend that it is your top priority in that moment to serve with grace?

Setting intentions doesn't only affect what outcomes we have, what we receive or what we achieve. They also serve others when we are true to ourselves. You get to decide if setting intentions is something that you'll just keep thinking about or something that you'll embrace and get serious about.

If you stay at the day-dreaming stage, you'll probably still be sitting waiting for something to happen. If you're serious though, you'll be out there helping the universe to join up the dots and you'll have some spectacular results.

You will need to show up; you will still need to do the work. But my, oh my, when you do, that's when the magic happens.

All the parts of a feature length movie are important, and each and every layer still requires attention so that the overall movie is magnificent. If you put in the effort and get each of these layers operating fully, you'll love the outcome.

It is my intention that you'll fall in love with selling. That you'll not only get to LOVE SELLING, you'll also discover the joy and ease of selling without having to sell out. To sell freely and without ever having the need to compromise your values in order to gain a sale is utterly sublime. I'd like to show you how it can be fun.

Chapter 3: sElling – ENTER THE SALE

The necessary preparation in order to deliver excellence

'It is thrifty to prepare today for the wants of tomorrow.'

Aesop

Let's enter the sale and start selling.

There are a number of elements that you will need to get into place so that when you do engage with your client you will be able to fully enagage and give them your full attention and focus. This is fundamental to being ready to serve. There's nothing quite like good solid preparation to get everything off to a great start.

In any interaction and in every sale, there are three main elements: a Before, a During and an After.

I'm going to show you how you can LOVE SELLING in each of these and how you can achieve this without having to sell out.

Throughout the S-E-L-L-I-N-G process we're going to dive into each of the steps and uncover the delight and reward of what true service can bring and in doing so we will maximise the sales experience for both our clients and ourselves. This means that you'll be best placed to serve your clients with wholehearted passion, integrity and help them solve their problems with ease.

I'll cover some communication skills which will support you in that process. I'll also go into some of the science behind why we do what we do. We'll then pull it all together so that you have a robust sales process and a clear pathway to successful and integrous SELLING.

'E'ntering the Sale:

Entering the sale is all about preparation. It's about creating the time and space so you have a solid platform on which to be the greatest version of you. This is the ground work, the stuff that separates you from the norm; it's the glue that holds everything together so that you add value.

It's the Before of the Before, During and After.

So what's it all about?

- Knowledge
  These are the 3 Ps of knowledge. This is about building your knowledge so that you create the best possible support for yourself, and in doing so add real and lasting value to any client or business.

- Sales Aids

  We're going to have a chat about sales aids. What they are, why have them and where to find them.

- Appearance

  We're going to get up close and personal about personal appearance; how and what does good look like, and why?

- Mind-Set

  We're going to take a peek into the amazing world of mind-set; the huge reservoir of pure potential we all have. This is your own personal powerhouse which can take you down or elegantly drive you up, in each and every moment of every day.

- Approach

  Let's get the ball rolling so you can decide what suits you best, how to get started and how to determine your approach. Once you're prepared and ready to make the most of the time with your client, we'll examine how you gain respectful control in a super-efficient and conversational manner so that your client meetings or sales conversations are productive and useful to your client and you.

Apart from being physically ready and prepared to enter the sale, I want us to get clear on how seemingly unrelated behaviours and events can, both positively and negatively, impact your sales process and therefore influence your client. These seemingly unrelated matters can determine the outcome of the interaction you have with your client so they're important to get right.

Knowledge

How do you build your knowledge in a consistent and on-going basis so that you have everything you may need when you engage with your client?

You will be surrounded with a number of avenues in which to find help and support in the work that you do, and yet so often the resource right in front of you is so easy to miss or not take seriously.

So how can you develop your knowledge?

It's as likely to be Google as it is a colleague or mentor, a representative from a supplier of yours or a product itself. It can be, and is, anyone and anything that can help support you deliver value and expertise to your client.

Like all elements of sales, it's an on-going process of determining what may be important to your client and therefore what is important to you. Your job is to help your client solve a problem, which means that you have a requirement to know a range of potential solutions to help them achieve this. Whether you're in the business of supplying parts for aircraft, physiotherapy for a client with a sports injury, face cream to rejuvenate, or cream to block out the sun, you need to know what your client may need and want in order to be able to serve them properly.

Regardless of your employment status – whether you are employed by a corporate or a small local business, run your own business, are a sole trader or self-employed – this rule still applies. You need to know your stuff. Knowing your stuff will be critical to adding true value to your clients. Investing the time it takes to prepare means that when you enter the sale, whether that takes the form of a client consultation, a sales call, or any sales meeting or conversation, you are ready and prepared to serve.

So how do you do this?

The 3 Ps

The easiest and most effective way is to start with the 3 Ps – that's People, Places, and Products.

People

Who in your immediate network can help you increase your knowledge and awareness? This could be the colleague sitting next to you, your line manager or a friend. It could be your co-workers who you meet at the monthly sales meeting or alternatively the person who is ranked as the top sales person within the organisation.

One thing is for sure, even if you are a sole trader; there will be people in your immediate network that will be able to impart knowledge to you. This could be product knowledge, industry awareness, effective processes and procedures or anything that supports you being your best version.

Now this doesn't have to be a formal 'let me sit you down and extract as much information as possible' meeting with an individual, although it could be. But one thing is for sure, if you do not cultivate an appetite for increasing your knowledge and building your own awareness, you won't. At a non-sales level that may be fine, but of course you are unlikely to add the highest possible value when you engage with your client, which from a sales perspective, is unacceptable.

Find the people who can help boost your knowledge and engage with them. Make this a continual process of learning and self-development.

Places

We are surrounded by a plethora of information. The internet is available to many of the seven billion humans on this planet; use it. Use the forums that you have available to you so that you increase your knowledge about your trade, your profession, your industry and the specific products and services that you offer.

Viewing your own company website and social media sites will give you a massive download of information. Do this regularly, as they are frequently updated, upgraded and amended, and you will be stunned at the level of knowledge that has been available to you all along. You'll also be surprised at the new layers of information you absorb each and every time you do this exercise.

If you are a sole trader or a private business owner, still visit your own website. Even though you created it, your focus may have changed and what you remember to be a key offering may not be any more or you may have become distracted from your core offering. Even more importantly, you may have forgotten the energy of your own enthusiasm since you first developed and built your site.

Trade shows, social media groups, and the numerous platforms available for like-minded people are all ideal places for you connect with so that you increase your knowledge in a consistent and continuous manner. Some you'll love, others you'll discard but go searching for them – and often. The amount of valuable information, tutorials and various learning platforms available is stunning.

It'll help you become more up-skilled, more knowledgeable and more aware, which in turn will add enormous value to your clients.

Products

Being aware and informed of the benefits of the products and services that you offer is absolutely essential. Depending on the level at which you operate within the organisation your grasp of product knowledge will be critical to how effective you can be in actively and enthusiastically promoting them.

Knowing the technical specification of your products and services is of course useful. Understanding what they can actually do for a client is even more important.

Sales Aids

What do you have available to you that will help your clients at the point of sale?

Brochures, demo kits, products, samples, presenters, video guides?

I recently worked with a great group of guys whose job it is to design, specify and install central heating products in the domestic market. The core product of a central heating system tends to be a rather unsightly, cumbersome boiler, which, to the uninitiated, looks pretty much like a big white metal box. Not exactly a product that is visually aspirational.

In order to design and specify replacement central heating systems these representatives visit their clients in their homes. So that they could make it more interesting for their clients, they started to take along some of the smaller heating products and components to show them. They chose the more attractive items that may not be previously known to their clients – such as various smart technology items that can give a client greater control over their fuel consumption and so forth. Clients are able to see, touch and feel these ancillary products and are now far more engaged than they were previously.

Very quickly clients appeared more relaxed, more involved, more informed and therefore more in control of a process they often knew very little about. It served those clients having those smaller items to see, touch and feel. It also served and boosted the whole process of helping the client buy what they truly wanted and needed and, ultimately, have what was important to them installed in their home.

Use your sales aids in a fashion that truly builds value for your clients.

Whether you are in the central heating business, the beauty business, banking or retail, you will almost always have some kind of product or service that can be tangibly demonstrated or shown to your client so that they can start to understand the true benefit for themselves.

Ask yourself why someone would need your product or service. What will it do for them? What problem will it solve? How can you demonstrate this to your client?

What I mean by this is, what sort of problem would someone have in order for my product to be an ideal solution?

If your products and services genuinely don't solve a problem, then walk on by. Find something else to do. After all, we are helping clients to solve problems they have, we are helping them to choose wisely when they buy, we're not flogging stuff.

I have yet to find a product or service that does not answer someone's problem, somewhere. It starts with viewing everything you have available to you in your portfolio as another method of solving a client problem. In doing so, you will quickly shift the energy to that of serving your clients rather than desperately trying to flog stuff to them.

We'll cover more of this later but for now use whatever sales aids are available to you, seek them out, be curious, be inquisitive, develop and increase your appetite for knowledge.

It'll serve you in being fully prepared to enter the sale and it'll delight your client when they know they can trust you to be able to help and guide them.

Appearance

Appearance matters. The hippy in me really wishes it didn't. But it does.

Making sure that you are prepared is a basic requirement in sales. Whether it is having what you need to hand, the condition of your equipment, the appearance of your sales aids or your personal appearance, they will do one thing: they will have an effect on how you are perceived. You are representing your brand, so what impact do you want to have and how do you want to be perceived? Whatever is being reflected is a reflection of your brand.

Consider all the equipment you use in your day to day life in sales – things like quote pads, your tablets and phones, brochures, samples, displays, demonstration kit, tape measures or whatever else you may use or need when you engage with your client face to face. Are they in good repair? Are they fit for purpose? Are they clean and do they look presentable?

The answers to the above questions will, without question, have an impact on your sales results. And in a subtle way, will have an impact on your customer satisfaction. Inexperienced sales folk may avoid paying attention to these seemingly small details, but they do so at their peril, and will often wonder why their clients don't respond to them in a way that they had hoped.

There are a couple of areas that really deserve our attention.

Attire

We all have different views on dress code: what is smart, what's casual and what professional looks like – and that's not going anywhere near what works for our quirky personalities. Amongst all of that is an important middle ground where we present ourselves in a manner that is conducive to clients wanting to do business with us.

The many layers that build up to customer satisfaction are complex. Amongst these are some of the finer and more subtle layers which can act as unnecessary distractions if we are not aware of them. Our personal appearance and the appearance of any equipment or sales aids we use is a non-verbal communication of who we are.

So the question we should ask ourselves is, how do we wish to be perceived?

It's a question worth considering seriously because your attire will be a huge non-verbal communication indicator to your client. Your clients' perception of who you are will be, in part, based on your appearance.

So what does good look like? What does 'smart' mean? What does 'businesslike' mean? What's appropriate in your industry?

If it's an outward appearance of so called perfection, then regrettably we may fall a little short of the mark but, in reality, the fact remains that considering how we are perceived is still important.

Rightly or wrongly, our appearance plays a huge part in this. Taking care of our appearance could be as simple as making sure that we are dressed in a manner that is fit for purpose. Your job will often dictate what you wear, which is quite straightforward; but what about the other aspects of your dress code and general appearance?

Just as the appearance and condition of the equipment and props you use gives your client an insight to what you consider to be acceptable, so does your physical appearance.

Many of the businesses that I've worked with over the years, both large and small, have opted for some kind of corporate wear. These have ranged from formal all the way through to practical and casual. Having a corporate image can be subtly reassuring to a client and can also evoke pride in your workforce. Let's face it; you're going to have an image no matter what, so it's worth considering what you would prefer it to be.

I recently worked with a client who has a large network of installers. As I came out of their head office building one morning I couldn't help but notice the installation team who were leaving their depot. There must have been at least thirty of the team there and they looked amazing, all dressed in casual but immaculate polo shirts and dark combat like trousers. They were ready and prepared to carry out their day's work. All the vans were immaculate, clean, and well cared for. In that moment I felt the full force of their brand. I was proud that I worked with an organisation that had such high standards and I'm pretty sure that every client they saw that day would have felt the same. It's a powerful non-verbal communication.

In my own experience of being a customer, I notice how this is true.

Every month I get a facial, every month I'm welcomed by the clinic staff who I've known for ten years. Apart from the smiles on their faces, they all wear a version of a clinic uniform. It's not an official uniform but you definitely know they're wearing the brand. The clinic has five people working there but they all, without exception, wear that brand with pride. I've tried other clinics over the years just to see what else was out there but each time I come back to this one. I love being welcomed with a big smile and a team that look aligned, ready for work and efficient. They look like they are ready to do business, and they are. Their behaviour is in complete alignment with their image.

When someone new joins the team, they too don the clinic colours and everyone is clear who works there and who is a client. We all enjoy the certainty of it all.

I'll cover more about certainty in Chapter 7, but suffice it to say that corporate wear or whatever you wear will have an impact on your client.

Thinking about what you wear and how you present yourself is therefore important.

Depending on the industry you are in, crazy wild quirkiness may be perfect. But before you step out to meet your client, do take a little time to consider what your clients' perception of you might be when you walk through the door.

It is your non-verbal communication and a serious non-verbal statement that you're making. Your clients' perception of you will influence how they connect with you or in fact if they connect with you at all.

Appropriate

Now what happens if you don't have a uniform or corporate wear or your business doesn't have any guidelines? It then simply comes down to what's appropriate or put another way; what is fit for purpose?

Is your appearance and how you present yourself fit for purpose?

Would you wear your pyjamas for a day at the beach? Would you plough a muddy field in your slippers? Although silly examples, I'm hoping you get my point.

Being appropriately presented means that your appearance won't be a distraction. You probably want to be taken seriously; you probably would like to engage with your client at the deepest possible level and get to the heart of the matter with regards to their needs. It's a darned sight easier if you simply present yourself in a manner that is fit for purpose than make some kind of statement. Personal appearance statements are possibly for other times.

By that I don't mean to diminish yourself, I do not mean numbing out, or dulling down the essence of who you are, or even considering not being you. Far from it. Just take some time out to consider your clients' likely perception of you as you walk through the door.

Is your presentation appropriate and fit for purpose? Is the way in which you present yourself supporting the outcome that you want to achieve?

So this is not so much about personal style as it would first seem; this is about supporting the outcome of what it is that you want to achieve and then, if necessary, adapting your personal style to compliment and align with that outcome.

Everything that you do, everything that you present, everything that you portray to your client will be giving a nonverbal message of how you wish to be perceived.

What might their perception be? Is it what you intended it to be?

Mind-Set

The topic of mind-set is probably one of the most fascinating subjects in terms of what is actually possible for human achievement. We've all heard amazing, against all odds accounts of exceptional achievement which were mainly attributed to an individual's particular mind-set.

Our mind-set will determine our depths and our heights. Navigating our lives successfully starts with our own mind-set.

They say – what you think about, you bring about.

Imagine a lemon, a fabulous, juicy lemon that's right in front of you now. You notice its bright yellow colour, you pick it up and bring it towards your nose and smell the fragrance on the skin, you scrape your finger nail across the skin of the lemon and the zest is revealed followed by a ping of juice from the lemon.

It makes your eyes water as it shoots up against your face. Now take a small bite of the lemon, notice how it feels on your tongue and now notice the saliva building up in your mouth as you bite in further.

So where's the lemon? Many people reading this will probably now have more saliva in their mouths than a minute ago. The longer you go with the lemon scenario the greater chance you'll have of truly experiencing the lemon. You'll be able to see the lemon, hear your finger nails scrape along the peel to reveal the zest, feel the splashing ping of the juice as it shoots up to your face, and taste it in your mouth. If you don't like lemon it may be unpleasant, if you do like lemon you'll enjoy the freshness of the fragrance and the sharpness of the taste. You'll almost certainly have more saliva in your mouth, just as you would if you had the lemon right there in your hand. But there is no lemon; it's only an exercise about a lemon. Yet your brain, and mine, reacted as though the lemon was right here, right now.

Your brain, and mine, cannot differentiate between what is real or unreal. Even though there is no lemon near you, you still have a physiological response to the thought that you are biting into a lemon. We are hard-wired to experience in this way.

That's one of the reasons why music can be so moving or motivating, why laughter can be so contagious. It's also why, when many of us think about our school days and remember chalk scratching down the school blackboard, we will wince and shiver at the mere thought of it. It's a sound that still rings in many of our ears. There's no blackboard here and yet we still have the physiological response to that sound.

We are extraordinary creatures. We can simply think of something and recall what it looked like, what it sounded like, the smell and all the feelings associated with the experience – and we can do it right now, on demand. We can call it up to conscious thinking on demand.

Knowing that this inherent skill is available to you, whenever you choose it, is hugely helpful to us sales folk.

Imagine for a moment just how empowering this is for you. You can ensure that you always have a choice as to how you receive your client. You always have a choice, in each and every moment, to engage with a client in a positive, clear and resourceful manner.

In order to become highly effective at managing, or even mastering your mind-set, there really needs to be an overriding desire to master your own feelings and internal dialogue. Once you've set that intention, be prepared to be honest enough with yourself when you slip from time to time – because you will. No matter how expert you are at this, no matter how experienced, you will slip from time to time, we all do. But reducing the frequency and the depth of the slip is extremely helpful, especially in sales.

Having the tools and techniques to catch yourself, and self-rectify in that moment, is something that is part of the ongoing development and life of a successful sales person.

The harsh reality is that selling doesn't always go to plan – no matter what anyone tells you. Not everyone will buy from you and you won't always know why. Sometimes you will disconnect with your client and you won't necessarily know why. You may, sometimes, just simply not do a good job. But you need to know why and you need to be honest enough with yourself to get back on track quickly.

How you choose to behave is really your business. No external event can be responsible for how you choose to behave – taking responsibility for your own development in this particular area of your life as a sales person will have a significant impact on the level of your success.

How do you maintain your state such that you don't have the 'monkey' on your back?

This question will need to be your go-to point regularly. This is not just a one-off 'got-it' learning – it is the kind of personal enquiry that you will ask yourself continually and then modify your thinking accordingly.

One thing is for sure, whatever is preoccupying your thoughts will find its way into your behaviour and ultimately into your results. Making it your priority to be aware of what's going on in your thinking will make a difference to your results.

A number of years ago I had what many would consider to be a fabulous job. I held a leadership position within a business that was considered to be the market leader in its industry. Life was good. I enjoyed being part of the leadership team. I had worked hard to ensure I had a great management team. I had good relationships with the various departments within the business. The members of the sales force were fun, hardworking people who were committed to the business. The sales were rolling in and life was pretty tickety-boo.

And then I made the decision to leave. I had been approached by a couple of entrepreneurs who wanted me to join them in a start-up. Apart from the fact that my ego kicked in and I was hugely flattered, being involved in a start-up very much appealed to me. It all seemed so exciting and adventurous.

Well, exciting and adventurous it was not. I'll fast forward to spare you the pain but it was a nightmare. Your average horror movie in full Technicolor – it was just awful. Nothing was as I had been promised, funding was sparse and then fully retracted and frankly the whole thing was ordinary in the extreme.

Let me tell you that for the weeks and months that followed I had to micromanage my mind-set. And I mean *micro* manage it.

There will be times where all your power and skill will have to be poured into simply getting up. There will be times where every ounce of energy you have will be required just to show up. Do it. Eventually whatever took you offline will pass and you will get back to normality. Putting these kinds of events to one side and showing up for your client in a fresh and open manner is what your client deserves.

Knowing that you have the ability to manage your mind-set so that you can get up and show up doesn't mean that at times it won't be difficult and challenging. But all you need is a five-minute window of self-correction for it to start the process of healing and of getting you back up on your feet to face another day. There will be external events that are a shock to you and you may be reeling for a while, needing time to heal, but for the most part of each and every day you can manage your thinking such that you can be present enough, for long enough, to do what needs to be done to get the job done well.

You can then go home and pull the duvet over your head; but in the moment of stepping into your sales call or meeting, put it aside and get to work. Your client deserves that from you and you'll heal quicker if you do.

Approach

Now that you are physically and mentally prepared to meet your client, how can you make sure you get your approach in tune with your client and get the first five minutes of the meeting rocking?

It goes without saying that you'll almost certainly want to maximise the time you have with your client so there are some key points to consider prior to any client meeting.

What is the most useful meet and greet for me?

What is my ideal meeting structure?

What tone would I like to set for the meeting?

How can I set the expectations for the meeting?

In other words how can you respectfully control how the time is spent during the

SELLING

ENTER THE SALE

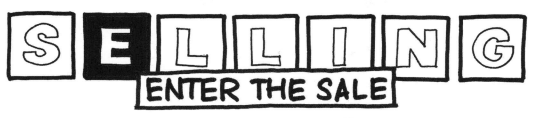

KNOWLEDGE

PEOPLE

PLACES

PRODUCTS

SALES AIDS

APPEARANCE

MINDSET

APPROACH

meeting such that comfortable and productive structure is achieved for your client and you?

So let's take a look at a couple of areas that can help you achieve this.

1. Maximise your meet and greet and,

2. Deliver an effective agenda set.

By mastering these two areas you will gain respectful control of the meeting. You are less likely to become distracted and, even more importantly, your client is also less likely to become distracted. This means you'll have the foundation for a successful and productive meeting where the time available is optimised.

Meet and Greet

It is said that you only get one chance to make a first impression. It is well documented that we make that decision within the first few minutes, sometimes even seconds, of meeting someone.

Whether we like it or not – first impressions count.

So taking time to think about how you want to be perceived and how you are actually being perceived is a valuable and important step towards ensuring that your client meeting is positive and meaningful.

It's all about perspective – yours and theirs.

Your perspective:

- What impression do you want your client to have of you?

- And why?

Your client's perspective:

- Who is this person in my office?

- Is this person a good fit for us, our culture, and our brand?

- Why should I trust this person with this important project?

- Why should I believe him/her?

Bridging any gaps:

- How are you going to ensure that your client perceives you as you intended?

- Knowing that you are an expert in your field – how can you ensure that your client perceives these positive and useful traits in you?

- How can you positively demonstrate that your expertise and knowledge can be of benefit to your client?

Deciding on these factors is important so that you can get the meeting off to a positive and productive start.

So how do you introduce yourself? What is your opening statement? What 'headline statements' do you want the prospect to remember? By headline statement I mean a short, memorable and meaningful introduction. This is a personal choice. Something you will need to decide for yourself.

I remember when I was Sales Director for a business that manufactured furniture.

It was at a very busy time of the year when a man, who I'd never met before, contacted our office requesting a meeting with me. He was offering a broad range of training services.

His call was highly opportune. It just so happend that it came at a time shortly after we had highlighted that we could really do with some additional help in this area. Our growth plans had been pretty fierce and although we were doing a pretty good job in ensuring our induction training program was robust, it was starting to show signs of creaking at the seams. We really needed some additional support so I was pleased when, quite out of the blue, this man had requested a meeting with me.

On the day of the meeting he was ushered into my office a little early as I was elsewhere in the building. I arrived at the time we had arranged to meet and stretched out my arm to shake his hand and introduce myself. As I did this, he did the same. As his hand reached out to meet mine he launched into his introduction,

'Hello, darling. I'm the best sales trainer you'll ever meet.'

I felt like saying, 'Hello, Houston. We have a problem.'

Needless to say, he might well have been the best sales trainer I would ever meet but I can tell you that I will never, ever know. It was a short meeting. The only topic of conversation was about him. He repeatedly told me how fabulous he was and I stayed polite and drew the meeting to a close pretty quickly.

In case I'm not being clear – for me, his introduction was not helpful: it was silly and it irritated me; he didn't have the elegance or personality to carry it off. So I shut down – fast!

He'll never know that I had looked forward to meeting him because we had a real and present need for some training assistance, but he turned me off and shut me down with that introduction. I couldn't get past it. I think the only reason I continued with the short meeting is probably due to some possibly misplaced value on having manners. It wasn't a good use of my time – or his.

First impressions count – so make those few seconds count. Don't do weird. Don't do quirky. Just be a regular person who is meeting a client. It may sound a little old fashioned, but 99% of the time it really works.

Food for thought

First impressions are a two-way street. So give some thinking time to how you manage the first impression you have of your client?

Are you aware of any judgements you may have made?

Many years ago I was working as an assistant in a large showroom. We sold fitted bedroom furniture. It was my job to make appointments for our designer to visit clients in their home with a view to measuring up and selling the bedroom furniture installation. It was late one Saturday afternoon – just before closing time – and was raining like crazy outside, when a young guy came into the showroom. No one ever visited the showroom this late on a Saturday afternoon. Well, no one who was serious anyway. I had wondered if he was just getting out of the rain as there was a bus stop right outside my showroom door. Perhaps he was just sheltering from the heavy onslaught of rain while he waited for a bus.

He was much younger than our usual serious clients. He wore ripped jeans (before ripped jeans were the norm) and a T-shirt that had frays around the bottom hem. Definitely someone just getting out of the rain I thought.

I was not interested in dealing here. You're kidding me! Ten minutes to closing time, a guy with ripped clothes, raining outside. No, I was sure that this wasn't a proper client. So I did the false smile and 'Can I help you?' thing.

'Yes,' he replied 'I'd like to arrange for a designer to come and see me. Tonight.'

Oh for crying out loud, we never ever have designer appointments on a Saturday night, stop wasting my time I thought. I secretly didn't want to make the appointment but frankly didn't know how to get out of it.

I won't bore you with any further rambling but I begrudgingly made the appointment, he left my showroom and I phoned it through to my designer. I was relieved when he picked up because I really wanted to explain how I had been forced to make the appointment for that evening. I just couldn't refuse a client requesting an appointment; but I felt sure it was going to be a waste of time. He wasn't the kind of person who buys our fitted furniture and so forth. As a favour to me, my designer agreed he would go to the client that night as appointed.

The following morning I was shocked and rather embarrassed at my pre-judgment. That scruffy client had bought six fitted bedrooms. Most clients only buy one or maybe two. I was blown away. The designer told me that he was actually a significant player in the music business; he and his wife had the most beautiful upscale home and wanted to complete their furnishings with fitted bedroom furniture. He had been dashing back home at the end of a day out, saw the showroom open and just dropped by.

Since that day, I have never knowingly pre-judged again.

Beware of your opinions. You almost certainly do not know the full details yet and you could be wrong in your judgement. I was.

Setting an Agenda

Engaging in a productive and meaningful way with a clear understanding of how your client can benefit from your products and services which relate to their specific needs, is the cornerstone of customer satisfaction and should be considered best practice for all sales people.

To this end, it is imperative for you to clearly lay out what you'll cover during the meeting. In other words, setting an agenda very early in the meeting.

Setting an agenda is the easiest and most sensible way to gain a level of respectful control especially for the time you spend time with your client.

Mastering this important step within your sales process not only starts to demonstrate your integrity by doing what you say you're going to do; it also assists in satisfactorily meeting the objectives of both your clients and yourself, for the time spent together.

Setting an agenda is a simple but powerful statement made by you in order to set the intention for the meeting. Very simply to state what you'd like to cover within the time available. This is always client-centric.

Depending on your selling environment, consider including some or all of the following in your agenda set.

- So that I can help you, may I explain what would be helpful to cover today? And then list them.

- In order to give you an accurate quotation, there are a few things we need to do. And then list them.

- I'd like to ask a few questions to find out what you need and what is important to you.

- If it's ok with you, I'll take some notes while we're talking so I capture everything and don't miss anything.

- I'll explain any potential savings you can make.

- I'll explain the solution we come up with.

- This usually takes about xxx minutes or so. Does that sound okay?

You will now have an obligation, and have respectfully earned the right, to deliver against the statements above that were promised and agreed.

Each statement within your agenda set should have a specific purpose and each is linked to a stage of your sales process. Each stage of the sales process is designed to create value within the visit.

For example, if you have specific payment options that you want to cover, include that in the agenda set.

Whatever you believe will add value, assist your client and serve the sales process; include it in your agenda set. That way you'll have created structure, and commitment that you'll be covering these items during that specific meeting.

It'll keep you on track but more importantly it will give certainty to your client that they know what's going on and what's likely to come next, which is likely to make them feel freer to let you know if they're short of time, or help you to get to the parts that are of particular importance to them.

Setting an agenda is an enabler for a smooth sales experience for you and your client. It's a simple act that has a huge impact. Leave it out and you'll find your meetings will run over, you'll get muddled up, perhaps distracted and lose your thread. Do it, and you'll have structure, your client will feel in control, they'll know how to pace themselves, they'll know what to expect throughout the meeting and everyone can relax and get down to the business at hand.

Chapter 4: SELLING – LEARNING

Learning about your client so that you can serve with grace

Learning is the beginning of wealth.
Learning is the beginning of health.
Learning is the beginning of spirituality.
Searching and learning is where the miracle process all begins.

Jim Rohn

Being open to learning about your client and what needs they may have is central to good quality communication. In sales and as always, also in life, the quality of our communication is central to how successful we are at managing the ebb and flow of our interaction with others.

How can we possibly help or serve a client if we don't understand what they need, what they want and what's important to them?

Having a genuine interest in learning about the needs of your client will therefore obviously stand you in good stead when the time comes for you to offer your solution to whatever their needs may be.

How could a client consider your solution if it doesn't meet their needs? They just wouldn't be interested.

Establishing your clients' needs is at the very heart of your job, so learning how to establish their needs, create and hold good quality, time bound conversations, will enhance your sales call, your meetings or any interaction with your client.

Why is it important to do so? How else could you help your client if you don't know what's important to them? Be that in terms of products and services, or what they personally need. Put another way, what they may need emotionally, to help them feel safe and comfortable enough to buy.

You will need to dedicate some of the time spent with your client to establish their true needs – both product and emotional. What do they want and why? What do they think they need and why? What's really important to them and why?

Fact finding is critical so that you can accurately offer an appropriate and well thought through solution. Without a real interest in your client and without establishing their true needs a couple of things are likely to happen.

1. You will blind them with science about your products and services. Your client will become bored and disengaged. They will shut down. They will not buy unless you happen to stumble into mentioning something that they may want or need. It will be down to chance, and will most likely be exhausting for you and your client.

2. You will very likely offer up a solution that is not the best or most appropriate solution for your client. At best it won't be compelling and at worse it will be simply wrong for your client. Your client, feeling short-changed, will withdraw to think about it. They will not buy.

I'll cover the whole topic of needs and how they are created in great detail in Chapter 7 but for now, let's talk about talking. How can you establish your customers' needs with your verbal communication? How can you serve so that the highest good is achieved?

How can you open up the conversation and help your clients solve their problems with your products and services?

The answer lies in the quality of your questions, which will determine the quality of the information you receive as answers.

So let's take a look at some great conversational lines of enquiry that will provide you with the platform to create good quality and meaningful conversations with your client.

Let's get talking about talking.

More specifically let's talk about five specific questioning techniques which have proven to be highly effective in any sales environment.

Five questioning techniques

- Open questions

- Closed questions

- Alternative questions

- Recall questions

- Key word questions

Open Questions

These are questions that open up, and often start or extend, the conversation. Open questions give you the opportunity to encourage more dialogue and expand the conversation in a particular direction. By expanding the conversation you will easily establish further detail and information.

Open questions promote an explanation of a given situation. And in doing so you will create the opportunity to gain further information which will help you gain a better understanding of what is important to your client.

Open questions start with – What? When? How? Who? Why? Where?

Let's play:

What?

Travel agent: What kind of holiday are you thinking about?

Retailer: What got you thinking about replacing your computer today?

Business: What are you looking to achieve?

When?

Travel agent: When would you like to take your holiday?

Retailer: When were you thinking about installing your new computer?

Business: When did you want this work delivered?

How?

Travel agent: How long would you like your holiday to be?

Retailer: How many people will be using the headsets?

Business: How many products do you currently have in your portfolio?

Who?

Travel agent: Who is going on this holiday?

Retailer: Who may be using the new computer?

Business: Who will want to be involved in making the decision?

Why?

Travel agent: Why is flying with British Airways important to you?

Retailer: May I ask, why do you specifically like this brand of computer?

Business: May I ask, why do you currently use the single delivery service?

Where?

Travel agent: Where would you like to go on your holiday?

Retailer: Where will the equipment be most used?

Business: Where do you operate from?

Closed questions

Closed questions tend to promote a more direct response; mainly a 'yes' or 'no'.

As closed questions focus the attention, they are useful when establishing a conclusion to a given line of enquiry or questioning situation.

Travel agent: Is this the resort you were talking about?

Retailer: Do you like this colour?

Business: Is Monday afternoon convenient for you?

Like all questioning techniques, they are useful when used in the appropriate context. The different questioning techniques help the ebb and flow of conversation so that it flows; moves forward at the appropriate time and then reaches conclusion in a fashion that works for all concerned.

If you were going to start a conversation with a closed question for example, 'Can I help you?' you are most likely to get a simple Yes or a No answer. It's perhaps not the best way to engage with someone and start a conversation if you are pretty certain you'll get a stock Yes or No response.

However, there does come a time where you will want be sure of a particular point in order to move forward and let the conversation develop in other ways. Using a closed question to get specific clarification is very helpful. For example, 'Would you like milk in your coffee?' or 'Is twelve noon good for you?'

Alternative questions

This type of questioning promotes the choice between two or more options.

Alternative questions are useful when narrowing a decision about the various options.

Travel agent: Are you thinking of a resort or self-catering?

Retailer: Would you prefer your files located 'here' or 'here'?

Business: What works best for you; Monday or Wednesday?

What you're doing by using Alternative questions is giving choice. In other words, one will be chosen, just which one is it?

Recall questions

Recall questions refer to and bring to mind, a point made earlier.

> Travel agent: Do you remember earlier when I mentioned that I would cover the payment options?

> Retailer: Do you remember I spoke of our in-house brands?

> Business: Do you remember that I mentioned earlier that we have volume discounts available?

People will seldom disagree with you, as long as you have actually previously mentioned the point that you now wish to discuss.

Here are a couple of great uses for Recall questions which make life and sales conversations so much easier.

1. They enable you to carry out a part of your presentation, or a key explanation, at a time that is most relevant for the solution that you are proposing for your client. Travel agent: Do you remember earlier when I mentioned that we would need to complete visa forms for that destination? Well what I'd like to do now is complete those…

2. They are absolutely brilliant for commencing a follow up call.

    Business: Hi Mrs xxxx, its xxxx, I'm just calling as promised. Remember I promised that I'd give you a quick follow-up call today?

Key Word questions

Key word questions take their form from a statement made by your client.

The key to Key Word questions is that they are to be used sparingly. Otherwise they will appear contrived, which is yuk. Key Word questions are hugely powerful in really getting to the heart of the matter. Key Word questions seriously power up your communication.

For example, if a client says, 'Our computer has been a *nightmare.*'

The Key Word question is, 'When you say a *nightmare*, what do you mean by that?'

A Key Word question picks up a specific word or phrase that your client has used to describe their situation. It is a hugely effective way of asking for further clarification and delving deeper into what your client wants. Key Word questions are an excellent way of communicating with your client in their own words in order to go straight to the heart of the matter and establishing their needs.

Why is this so important? We all use linguistics as a method of communicating, yet we have varied understandings and unique experiences, which we express differently.

Let me explain. If there were twenty people in the room right now and I asked every person to share their most favourite vacation, some would say a skiing vacation, others would say being on a deserted island, others a tropical beach, and others would prefer a city tour. Each and every person would probably have a slightly different slant – even if two people said a tropical beach, those beaches are likely to have been explained differently.

Each one of us experiences our language in a unique way. Key Word questions get straight to your client's version of their experience.

If you are able to truly find out what your client wants and needs, and what's really important to them, you'll be able to determine how you may be able to help them. Key Word questions will enable you to do this quickly.

Client: We want an *amazing* holiday.

You: When you say an *amazing* holiday what do you mean by that?

In other words, what does 'amazing' mean to you? If you can really hear your client and find out what's important to them, then the quality of your meeting, the consultation, the session, or your sales call will be boosted in quantum leaps.

Apart from getting to the heart of the matter so that you can provide an appropriate solution, Key Word questioning also demonstrates active listening.

Being truly heard is one of the greatest gifts we can offer in conversation.

Can you imagine how great your client will feel if you truly hear them? Key Word questions can support that process and often enables your client to appreciate your attention to detail. They will welcome the opportunity to have a good quality conversation with you.

SELLING
LEARNING

OPEN QUESTIONS

WHERE...? WHY...? WHO..? HOW...? WHEN..? WHAT...?

CLOSED QUESTIONS

YES NO

ALTERNATIVE QUESTIONS

A B

RECALL QUESTIONS

EARLIER IN THE CONVERSATION

KEY WORD QUESTIONS

BLAH, BLAH, BLAH KEYWORD BLAH, BLAH KEYWORD...

SO, TELL ME MORE ABOUT YOUR 'KEYWORD.'...

Summary

Using these five questioning skills will enhance your conversation with your client. It will also make your conversations efficient and productive. Most clients do not have the time or the energy to spend hours in dialogue with you. Having the skill set to have deep, meaningful and efficient conversation with your clients that are timely and time bound will be far more productive for you and them. The energy will be lighter, they'll appreciate the time they have with you and you will build your relationship much quicker.

You will create and maintain the platform for a successful sales relationship with your client.

Chapter 5: SEL**L**ING – LISTENING

Tuning into your higher self and your clients

'Listen with the intent to understand, not the intent to reply.'

Stephen Covey

Being heard is one of the most fundamental yearnings we have as humans.

Listening is therefore one of the most powerful gifts we can offer a fellow human being. Listening to your client, and I mean really listening, is a powerful addition to your sales skills tool box. There are some environments where listening is a rare commodity; as ego fights ego the message that is waiting to be heard is lost, often forever. Eventually folk just shut down as it's no longer worth the struggle to be heard.

There's an art to listening that goes way beyond simply waiting for your turn to speak. Obviously in its most basic form, listening will enable you to establish what your client needs and wants. Whilst that is clearly important, I first want us to explore another kind of listening; the kind of listening that sometimes escapes us as we go about our busy, noisy, often time poor lives.

I want to talk about the art of listening to yourself.

Listening to yourself

When last did you truly listen to you? I mean really listen intently to the murmurings and whispers of your soul? Maybe never or maybe you've sidelined it due to busy schedules or other commitments.

I remember a significant breakthrough I had many years ago. It was on one of those powerful, defining moments that make it seem like it happened only yesterday.

I was attending a class on optimising personal energy. How we integrate our mental, emotional and spiritual bodies has always been of interest to me, I love most things metaphysical so I was really looking forward to taking the class. Wanting to ensure that I secured a good seat and an uninterupted view of the lecturer, I arrived early that morning. With my bag over my shoulder, I snuck into the classroom before anyone else had arrived. Or so I thought.

Across the room was a stunningly beautiful woman. She radiated the most calm and serene of energies. Her skin was like porcelain, she had dark, short hair and was immaculate in her dress. I was drawn to her. Even though she was seated toward the side of the class which was not where I wanted to sit, I felt compelled to sit beside her. And as I did, in a sweet, soft, American accent she said, 'Hi, I'm La Rue, and how are you today?' In that moment we became friends and we started to chat.

She worked with people who wanted to get clarity in their life and work decisions and had over the previous twenty years developed a proprietary method of cutting through the noise so as to get to this truth that lay within each of her clients. Slightly embarrassed that I wasn't really sure what she meant, I explored further. So how does this work, then? Her answer was one that has travelled with me ever since. She said, I help people truly listen to themselves. I help people really hear what their soul wants, what is at the core of their being. It sets them free to be who they really are and really want to be.

I was hooked.

Over the years, I've had the privilege to work with La Rue Eppler and we've become great friends and colleagues. But that day, all those years ago, as I walked into class I never dreamt it possible to actually 'listen' to me and establish what my soul wanted, what my soul was yearning for. I never imagined that I could learn how to listen to the whisper of my soul.

So why am I sharing this with you? Well, I immediately started the process of learning how to engage with myself the way La Rue teaches. What I discovered was a plethora of profound truths that had previously passed me by. One that was particularly powerful was a false belief I had been holding that I wasn't creative. For whatever reason, I had been lugging around the belief that I was not creative and therefore couldn't be, or even consider being, involved in creative things.

Once I realised how ridiculous and untrue this simple but profoundly damaging false belief was, I was shocked at the ramifications it had had in my life thus far. The unnecessary damage it had caused was now easy to plot back and I was surprised at how I had I kept reinforcing it throughout my life. I followed her process: I resolved and neutralised the false belief and let it go. I was now ready to fully embrace the fact that I am creative.

I am creative. I love creativity, I love to sort things out, I love to join up the dots, sometimes in my imagination and mainly in my work. I like to piece things together and I love to create a plan. I love sharing the plan and enjoying the success it brings.

I felt unburdened and free. Anything was possible. My sales life rocketed shortly after I owned and accepted my soul's yearning to be creative. Once I let go of the false belief that I was not creative, it opened the flood gates to my creativity. I flourished and as a result my sales team flourished; I instigated more creative projects in the years that followed than ever before. The joy was immense and still is. To this day it is at the core of who I am.

I listened to myself – I heard the whisper of my soul and acted upon it.

We spend so much time listening to others although arguably the most important dialogue is with ourselves. Yet listening to ourselves often gets put to the side.

I had been screaming out to myself for years but had chosen to ignore it and my true essence had been diminished, made to play small and often been snuffed out.

Take time out to listen to you – what do you really want and need? Be quiet for a moment – it takes practice but is well worth the investment of time. Hear you and hear what your soul's purpose is. It's whispering to you if you'll only just give it a chance to be heard. Deepen the discovery of who you really are and what you really want and you'll experience joy like never before.

As we saw earlier in the book, I recommend that you regularly have a meeting with yourself. I really am serious about this. Refine the art of listening to yourself so that eventually it becomes your go-to position for nourishment and direction. You know yourself so much better than you may think you do.

In sales, listening is quite possibly the most important skill to harness and cultivate.

This is a central truth of LOVE SELLING. It's the very essence of how to sell without selling out.

Selling is such fun and you don't need to sell yourself out in order to be great. So when you take time out to have a meeting with yourself, do something that you love: a walk in the countryside, a bike ride by the ocean, listening to music that you love; create that space and time to really get in tune with listening to yourself.

You have the answers within you. By allowing them to come to the surface, you can enjoy your wealth and abundance in the most spectacular way possible.

Listening to others

Being able to create the space and set the pace during a sales visit is an important skill if you have the intention of being open and listening properly.

I've already spoken of the importance of setting an agenda for all sales interactions. It will give you and your client the opportunity to pace yourselves during the time spent together. Furthermore, your communication will be even more effective should you demonstrate to your client that you have truly heard them.

This may be as simple as nodding your head in agreement to a particular point, but it can go much deeper than that if you truly want a deeper connection with your client.

Be mindful that active listening is an active and enhanced process of listening to someone. Patience is required on your part to listen in a non-judgemental and neutral way. In a busy and time poor world, it is common practice to jump in with an answer before someone has actually finished saying what they need to say.

Furthermore, it is even easier to jump in with an answer when you are a subject matter expert. As an expert in your field it is very easy to quickly join up the dots and tell your client what it is that they need. Although this is mostly positively intended on the part of you, the expert, this common behaviour actually has the opposite effect – it shuts your client down and valuable information is lost forever.

Allowing someone to complete what they are saying without interruption, learning how to feel comfortable with silences as your client internally processes their next question or thought, is all part of active listening.

It is actually quite difficult to master and something that must gain your full attention or you will suffer the consequences. If you don't hold the space for your client, you won't pick up on the finer detail and your questioning skills will be wasted. The outcome will often be a frustrated client and you are likely to fall into the trap of circumventing the conversation by presenting a solution that does not meet your client's needs.

If your client is polite they will probably tell you that they'd like to think about it. At worse your client will simply shut down.

There are many layers to needs, which I will cover in Chapter 7. For the moment, suffice it to say that you will miss all or most of them should you not fully practise active listening. Making the effort to remain present to what your client is saying, allowing them to fully express themselves whilst practicing active listening will always deliver far superior outcomes.

Listening to your client requires total concentration. It's all about them. You don't only listen with your ears. It's a visual, verbal, energetic means of taking in what and who someone is and exactly what it is that they are communicating to you. It's about their body language, the words they use and maintaining eye contact and connection so you capture every nuance that is being communicated to you.

Note-taking

Note-taking is a powerful boost to active listening. I've found it's always wise to seek permission to take notes if only to allow you some breaks in eye contact. But the power of note taking far exceeds what one first imagines.

It demonstrably supports you listening and it gives you the opportunity to capture key words and phrases. It will also give you the opportunity to identify specific needs that can be explored, clarified and if appropriate can be ultimately included in your solution.

Note-taking has a number of benefits.

You are obviously more likely to accurately capture all of the key requirements, thoughts, needs and salient points that have been made by your client. However, equally important for many clients is that it has the subtle and very positive effect of making them feel significant enough that you have made the effort to actually take notes. This further demonstrates that you are listening to your client and it supports your intention to ensure that all your client needs are met.

A while ago I worked with a team based in Scotland. They were part of a national UK sales force whose head office happened to be located about 500 miles away. For reasons that escape me, the leadership team in this organisation seldom bothered to make the journey to meet with them. In the process of getting to know the national sales force it made complete sense to me to travel to Scotland to meet the team myself.

The local management organised their sales meeting accordingly, I met everyone that morning and the regional sales meeting commenced.

Later that morning, at my previous request, the manager had created a slot on the agenda for me. I wanted to open up a discussion with the team. I had some key points I wanted to get clarification on and the team wanted to share some of the issues that were causing them concern.

Throughout the meeting I wrote notes to capture salient points. When it came to my slot on the agenda, I asked if they minded if I continued to take notes. Everybody nodded in agreement. During the open discussion, I had a few occasions where I had to stop briefly whilst I captured something that someone had raised but in the main I managed to capture a fair few pages of information and points that were important to me and the team.

The meeting concluded and I left that afternoon.

The following day the regional manager called me. Apparently the team were '*blown away*' by how refreshing it was that someone had not only visited them to seek their opinions but had actually listened to them. When I enquired further what they meant by this, he said that several team members had commented on the fact that I had been taking copious notes. They said that they knew I was listening to them because I had taken notes; furthermore, they, to a man, had the belief that I was taking them seriously.

I was taking them seriously anyway, of course, but it was my note-taking that had cemented their belief that I was to be trusted and cared enough about them to capture what they were saying and sharing during the meeting.

TO YOURSELF

THE GENTLE QUIET VOICE WITHIN

TO OTHERS

HOLD THE SPACE FOR YOUR CLIENT

ATTENTION ON THEM

WHAT THEY SAY AND WHAT THEY DO

TAKE NOTES

(AND ALWAYS ASK PERMISSION FIRST)

Over the weeks and months that followed, the change work that the Regional Manager and I managed to pull off was phenomenal. I firmly believe that it was in part due to the notes that I took that day. They had a great relationship with their Regional Manager but they didn't know me from Adam. In that moment I was accepted, trusted, and given a chance to share what I had in mind for the team and their progression.

Needless to say, that team rocked – partly because they were a great team who were managed well, partly that they were open and willing to consider different approaches, and also in part because my solution for them included and ticked off many of the needs that they had. If I hadn't taken notes that day, I would certainly have missed many of the points that were important to them. I wouldn't have been able to check in and refer back to my notes over the months that followed, which means that I wouldn't have delivered against them. Creating the platform for a solid connection with that team came from my note taking at that first meeting.

Note taking works on so many levels.

It promotes the fact that you are a trustworthy person from a trusted company and you take their business seriously. Your behaviour of active listening and note taking gives a positive message to your client that you want to get it right. It's another non-verbal method of showing you care about them and they are important to you. Later on you can use your notes to summarise the detail of what you've captured during the conversation with your client, which is yet another way of demonstrating that you understand what is important to them.

Using your notes to summarise the main points and replay them back to your client is an excellent method of confirming that you have a thorough and accurate understanding of what they want and need. It also helps to clear any misunderstandings, should they exist, which means that you can proceed to create a solution or relevant quote to meet their specific needs.

By enhancing your awareness of how powerful the non-verbal components of listening and note taking are within your client meeting, and once you add good quality questions, you will quickly start to make sense of how this all fits together to create an effective and productive means of communication.

Chapter 6: SELL**I**NG – INVOLVE

The energy of connection and collaboration

'The way you see people is the way you treat them, and the way you treat them is what they become.'

Johann Wolfgang von Goethe

How can you elegantly involve your client in the sales process? Why would you want to involve them at all?

Throughout the sales experience I wonder how much more pleasurable it would be for your client if they actually enjoyed the experience? In fact if your client enjoyed the sales experience, wouldn't that be more enjoyable for you. In fact might it be easier for everyone too?

Involving your client throughout the process is critical to building, and later maintaining, a productive relationship. If your client feels in any way disconnected at any stage it will not serve either of you and you will find it exceptionally difficult to establish what it is that they need and what's important to them. They are likely to shut down and disengage.

We've covered some questioning skills in Chapter 4 – that's part of the verbal communication.

So what about non-verbal communication?

Whatever you do non-verbally will either support or detract from your verbal communication. That being the case, how can you boost your verbal communication in a non-verbal way?

In Chapter 5 we covered active listening and note-taking. Now let's take a look at some more layers.

Everything that you are doing is directed towards giving your client the choice to 'buy' what it is that they want and need; this is an important point to keep at the forefront of your mind. Remember we're not 'flogging' stuff here.

So how else can you make the experience pleasurable and relevant for your client?

Let's take a closer look at some of those layers now.

- Non-verbal communication

- How we engage with clients

- Rapport

- Motivation

Non-verbal communication

We communicate by verbal and non-verbal means.

We've covered the specifics of effective verbal communication in the section on questioning techniques. It's now worth considering the impact of our non-verbal communication on the sales experience – for the sake of our prospect and ourselves.

How we engage with clients

The majority of our non-verbal communication is likely to be unconscious.

Whether you habitually tap a pen whilst in conversation with someone, smile easily or nod furiously when someone speaks to you, is mostly unknown to you – or at least, until such time as you choose to deconstruct your behaviours and examine them closely. This deconstruction is not necessarily something that is done each and every day but it is worth exploring and being mindful of, as the impact of your non-verbal interaction with your clients can be hugely supportive, or not, of the sales process.

Your non-verbal messages allow you to reinforce what you say out loud in words. You may nod in agreement with someone or shake your head in disagreement. These are all seemingly small gestures but they help to reinforce, or conversely contradict, what is being said within a conversation.

Non-verbal messages can also help to convey information about a person's emotional state – rolling your eyes towards the heavens or smiling instantly gives the person with whom we are in communication a perception of our 'feelings' regarding a particular situation. Of course this is only a perception so it will be generalised by the person you are communicating with. However, it is the most natural and immediate method of gaining feedback.

Reading your phone messages whilst with a client, may just give them the idea that you are distracted, uninterested, or some other event which is more important to you is taking your attention. This is probably an extreme example but hopefully it makes the point.

Your body language, your posture, and the eye contact you have or don't have, your facial expressions and personal space, all have an impact on the people with whom you are engaged with. It will therefore impact your communication. Being mindful of the effect your behaviour has on any given situation is a step towards considering how you choose to behave and the likely perception this will garner from your client.

You always have a choice… and so does your client.

Your client is at choice as to, which organisation they chose to partner with, which business they wish to deal with, which company they wish to become their supplier.

Being an open and authentic sales person means that being contrived or stilted in your communication with clients is not an option; yet if you are to serve your clients well, you will need to be mindful of how you are perceived and if necessary adjust your behaviours accordingly.

SELLING
INVOLVE

RAPPORT

CONGRUENCE
VERBAL & NON-VERBAL

MOTIVATION

TOWARDS   **AWAY-FROM**

Your non-verbal communication is as important as your verbal communication. It will serve to support everything that you say and do – if it is not in alignment with what you are saying, your clients will probably feel uncomfortable in your presence. That will not bode well when you present your recommendations for a solution to their need.

Rapport

Rapport: A close and harmonious relationship in which the people or groups concerned understand each other's feelings or ideas and communicate well:

She was able to establish a good rapport with the children
She had an instant rapport with animals

[Mass noun]: There was little rapport between them

The Oxford Dictionary

Given a choice, people buy from people they like and trust – fact.

No matter how good you think you are at your job, no matter how skilled, no matter how many years' experience you have or how knowledgeable you are, if you do not connect with your clients or you constantly disconnect, they will probably not like you and will potentially not trust you either. If this is the case, there will be a strong likelihood that they will be less inclined to choose you and your company for a solution to meet their needs.

It's worth noting that you definitely add value when you are good at your job, are skilled, have good solid experienced and are knowledgeable; so it's not just about being liked by everyone all the time. Being liked, by itself, is not enough to get the job done and it seldom delivers consistently high levels of customer satisfaction.

However, a combination of doing your job well with your client liking and trusting you is hugely powerful.

So it follows that the skill and ability of being in rapport with your client it is an important one.

The connection or rapport you have with your prospects will make a difference to your relationship, and it will influence their decision when they select the person or company to buy from.

Rapport is the platform for easy and effective communication.

Rapport is a state of perceived understanding with another. It is about you authentically matching yourself with another person such that both of you can relax and let go of the need to be guarded. If you are liked and trusted, it will almost certainly be easier for all concerned and you will be in a better position to assist your client with their project.

In sales you will be dealing with clients in varied environments so making the effort to gain and maintain rapport is important if you are to serve your clients well.

Being in rapport is an enabler. It enables good quality communication.

There are many ways in which to gain, build and maintain rapport and the great news is that, mostly, it happens quite naturally and at an unconscious level when you interact with others.

- Being appropriately cheerful and positive

- Initiating easy small talk – break the ice

- Offering an appropriate compliment

- Your body language

- Maintaining eye contact without staring

- Demonstrating that you observe what's important to the prospect

- Showing that you are interested

- Demonstrating that you are listening

- Being polite

- Being honest

- Being genuine

- Most important of all, being you!

Being aware of the impact that you have on others and modifying your behaviour accordingly, will not only assist you to be in rapport it will also help you to build and maintain that positive open connection with your client.

Motivation

What is motivation?

In its most simple form motivation it is best described as the pull away from pain and the urge towards comfort. It's the drive towards or away from something. It is a mechanism deep in the core of us humans.

I'm not talking about the "Whoop whoop!" stuff that often gets mistaken for motivation. That stuff is normally enthusiasm, which is fabulous in its own right, but not necessarily motivation.

> *Motivation: A reason or reasons for acting or behaving in a particular way.*
> *Escape can be a strong motivation for travel*
>
> The Oxford Dictionary

Motivation is what makes us humans take action. It's the driving force behind our actions. There are two basic elements to motivation – Away-from and Towards.

Away-from motivation:

Away-from motivation activates a behaviour that drives you away from a perceived discomfort.

If a tiger is chasing you, you may choose to run away from it as fast as you can. In other words, you are motivated to get away from the perceived danger or perceived discomfort. In other words you move away from the danger or discomfort as quickly and effectively as possible.

Towards motivation:

Towards motivation activates a behaviour that drives you towards a perceived comfort.

If you really want something, if it's really important to you, if it's really driving you, you will move heaven and earth to get it. Or you'll certainly give it your best shot. Consider the person who really wants to achieve a certain weight loss or fitness level. Buying that shiny new car. Providing for your famil or going flat out for that superb earning opportunity.

What do you want really badly?

You will probably be prepared to sacrifice some things in order to get an outcome you really want. In other words, if you really want a particular outcome, you will do whatever it takes in order to move towards achieving it.

Our motivation is the driving force behind our behaviours. As we feel even more strongly about a particular outcome our behaviours are modified in order to achieve what we want. They drive our actions.

We will always move **Away-from** a perceived lack of comfort, in other words pain, or **Towards** a perceived desired comfort, in other words pleasure.

Both are equally as powerful.

Please note that I say 'perceived' pain and 'perceived' pleasure. We all have our own versions, our own unique perception of what pain or pleasure is and therefore we will all have our own unique version of motivation – Towards and Away-from.

Of course there will be many generalisations, but at the very essence of each and every one of us there will be an exclusive set of motivations, both Towards and Away-from, that are unique to ourselves.

So why is this relevant to sales?

If we all have unique Towards and Away-from motivations, how might this play out when you engage with your client?

By ensuring that you take the time to create space and time to ask good quality questions of your client so that you can understand exactly what they need and want, you can be sure that what will drop out of the conversation is what's important to them. What's important to them will be the result of their motivation.

By using your questioning skills to ask your client what's really important to them you will have a far deeper and more meaningful conversation, and you will be far better placed to help them achieve whatever it is they need.

So how do you know what's motivating your client?

You establish what their needs are and why those needs are important to them. You take the time out to ask good quality questions in an elegant fashion so that you can help them achieve and fulfil those needs.

Chapter 7: SELLI**N**G – NEEDS

Establishing what your client needs

'No one has ever become poor by giving.'

Anne Frank

So far, I've made references to establishing your client's needs. I've mentioned numerous times that being able to offer an appropriate solution lies in how skilled you are at establishing what your client needs, what they want and what's important to them.

So what is a 'need' and how does it start? How does it develop and grow into an actionable outcome?

The birth of a need

According to the extensive research study by Huthwaite International, a need starts when an individual or group are no longer totally satisfied with the way things are. Anyone who is 100% satisfied with the way things are will not have the awareness of a need.

An event or an awareness of dissatisfaction will have to occur in order to trigger the start of the erosion of what was previously perceived as satisfaction. So the 'need', no matter how small, starts to develop as soon as that 100% satisfaction starts to be eroded.

Huthwaite's founder, psychologist Neil Rackham, suggests that the first sign of a need is a slight discontentment or dissatisfaction.

So how does this relate to your client?

You will want, and pardon the pun, 'need' to be concerned with both the Product Needs and Emotional Needs of your client. So what is their current challenge or issue and what are they dissatisfied with? Why are they dissatisfied?

Through good quality questioning you will establish the needs of your client. The product needs will assist you in your specific recommendations when you offer a solution and the emotional needs will assist you understand what this will do for, and what this means to, your client.

Both are important.

Remember the Towards and Away-from motivation? Something will be driving your client and their needs will be directly linked to that. When you establish what that is you will be able to help in the most exquisite way.

Types of needs

You will offer your client a far more appropriate solution if you have the intention of establishing all their needs, both product and emotional.

So often, only the product needs are discussed and explored. As a result when the time comes to offer a solution, it frequently falls short of what the client really wants.

PRODUCT

ECONOMY
EFFICIENCY
RELIABILITY
SECURITY

EMOTIONAL

SECURITY
SOCIAL
  ACCEPTANCE
ESTEEM
COMFORT
CERTAINTY

The emotional needs *have* to be satisfied otherwise your client is unlikely to be motivated to proceed with their purchase. It is in the emotional needs that client satisfaction resides – it's also where the joy of service resides.

The magic happens at the point where you are able to meet your client's product and the emotional needs. And it's the emotional needs being met which is what creates the emotion in your client so that they feel moved to buy.

How 'needs' are prioritised

Nature is great – it provides pretty much all of what we need in order to survive. From a psychological point of view, studies have shown that us humans have a series of 'needs' that, when satisfied, create the platform for our future needs to emerge.

Initially, our needs are around securing survival; once those are satisfied, we then go on to identify further needs which allow us to thrive. It is human nature to want to thrive.

Abraham Maslow, the great American psychologist, created the hierarchy of needs pyramid. This is a visual model that depicts how we prioritise meeting our needs.

Starting from the platform of the pyramid with the most basic of human needs, our physiological needs, he teaches us that once satisfied each subsequent tier presents the next level of 'needs' priority.

Starting with physiological needs: in its most basic form this is our need to have air so that we can breathe, food to eat and sleep to restore our minds and bodies. To eat, to sleep and to survive.

Safety needs: this is our need to have shelter, somewhere to lie down and rest whist being safe from harm. It's about our security, stability and our desire to have law and order.

So although the need for shelter is obviously important, when faced with a lack of oxygen, it becomes rapidly obvious that it is not as important as being able to breathe. Breathing, in other words our physiological need in this case, is a greater priority and therefore comes first in terms of the basic human need to survive. Once breathing is satisfied, then and only then, do we start to consider other needs we may have.

Social needs: these are our belonging and love needs. This is about belonging to the tribe, the need to be part of something bigger than ourselves, belonging to a group, a family, community, a network. Even a recluse will have this need, it just may be that they feel they belong to nature. There is a drive, deep within us, to belong and give and receive love.

Esteem needs are about the need for achievement. Independence, self-respect and the respect of others. It's about feeling that we offer something to the world, we contribute.

Lastly, the peak of the pyramid, self-actualisation. Maslow suggests that a mere 1% of humans will achieve self-actualisation. This is when we fulfil our potential, seek personal growth and become fulfilled in our life purpose. It suits me to believe that Maslow got the numbers wrong on this one and that self-actualisation is available to much more than just 1% of us.

So why is this important when helping clients?

While we are not pretending to be psychologists, it is useful to understand that we humans all have needs, which when met, or sufficiently met, create satisfaction. Once satisfaction is met we can easily consider the next 'need', and the process continues.

As sales people it is our job to establish what is important to our client, and as such, it is prudent to be aware that they will have needs that will be in an order of priority. Whereas it is highly unlikely to be as dramatic as life and death, or involve tigers chasing them, it is important to ascertain what your clients' needs are and why they consider them important, so that you can fully engage and assist them effectively.

Your client will be consciously aware of many of their needs. However, very often there are many more needs of which they are not yet consciously aware, such as the importance of safety, the mid and long term savings they could enjoy by the efficiency of products, various products which could make their life easier and more pleasurable, and perhaps products that can ensure greater peace of mind and enjoyment.

For you to offer relevant and appropriate advice and recommendations, knowing those needs and being able to meet most or all of them efficiently, will go a long way to enhancing the experience for your client and ultimately it will create a high level of client satisfaction.

By asking good quality questions you can effortlessly guide the conversation with your client to ensure that their needs are efficiently elicited. This will enable you to fully understand their specific situation and therefore enable you to propose a solution that meets their specific needs and requirements – both their product and emotional needs.

Implications of needs not being met

We've spent some time talking about establishing needs. I've also spent time highlighting that it's through asking good quality questions that you'll get into the muscle of what is creating the dissatisfaction within your clients' situations.

Knowing and doing all of this is great, but (and this is a huge big old 'but') only if you really understand the implications for your client should their needs not be met.

This is a biggie. This is the heart of any sale, any engagement, and any true level of service.

T H I S is B I G, folks!

This is the bit about really knowing what your client wants and needs at a deep level, from a Product and Services point of view and, very importantly, from an Emotional point of view.

What's truly important to your client, consciously or unconsciously, is what it means to them should their needs not be met. You truly 'getting' this is what creates the full picture of how you can help them.

If their needs aren't met, how will it make your client feel?

SELLING

NEEDS

PRODUCT

ECONOMY
EFFICIENCY
RELIABILITY
SECURITY

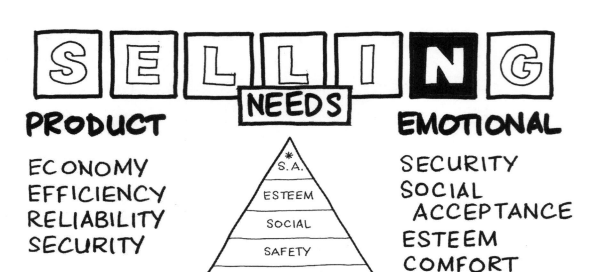

* S.A.

ESTEEM

SOCIAL

SAFETY

PHYSIOLOGICAL

*SELF-ACTUALISATION

MASLOW'S HIERACHY OF NEEDS

EMOTIONAL

SECURITY
SOCIAL
ACCEPTANCE
ESTEEM
COMFORT
CERTAINTY

NEEDS NOT MET

MEH.

Knowing the implications and what it means to your client if their needs aren't met is absolutely the most important element to every single engagement you have with them. After all, meeting those needs will avoid the implication occurring. This is where the client solution lies. This is where you get to help your client avoid whatever the implications are, should they not have their needs met.

So the final elements of your questioning and enquiry just have to be...

'So what is the implication of NOT fulfilling that need?' alongside finding out how that would make your client feel.

In a nutshell – if you don't get this right for your client:

What are the implications of not getting their need met?

How would it make them feel?

And my suggestion is that you tune into, 'How would it make you feel' if you haven't been able to isolate exactly why your client has this need in the first place?

Meeting the emotional needs of your client is by far the most important thing you can do for them. It's the most powerful driver of all. It's the very core of your job. It's where service really comes to the fore and you get to help your client.

Chapter 8: SELLIN**G** – GENUINE YES

Creating a safe and appropriate reason for your client to buy

'Always say 'yes' to the present moment ... Surrender to what is.
Say 'yes' to life – and see how life suddenly starts
working for you rather than against you.

Eckhart Tolle

When you've established what your client needs, what they want and what's really important to them you'll be well on your way to understanding what solution will meet their needs. Then, and only then, is the time to start presenting your solution.

So how can you do this in the most efficient and effective way?

Genuine Yes is about building an appropriate solution for your client's specific needs. It's about building value in everything that you do and demonstrating that value via your brand, products and services. It's about giving your client options, choices and prices and most importantly it's about giving your client the option to buy.

It doesn't end there though.

It's also about next steps. These could be about processing the order, explaining what happens next or following up on a meeting. Above all it's about trust, transparency and clarity so that their satisfaction level before, during and after their purchase is met, or even better still, exceeded.

So how do you do all of this?

Presenting your solution

Talking in Features, Advantages and Benefits, otherwise known as FAB, is an effective and proven way of presenting information about products and services so that the full power of your message is delivered in a highly efficient and productive way.

The FAB format highlights the 'value' of each product or service and can be used for any situation.

It will ensure that your client gets to understand the actual benefits that the product or service will give them. In other words, what's in it for them? This in turn re-iterates the value that the product or service will bring them.

Most people aren't particularly motivated to buy a toothbrush but they are motivated to have clean teeth. Most people aren't particularly motivated to have a bank account but they are motivated to keep their money safe with easy access. Most people aren't motivated to buy a dustbin but they are motivated to not have smelly rubbish lying loose.

It is seldom a particular product or service that will motivate your client – it is the benefit that the product or service delivers to them that motivates them. They want what it can do for them.

Once learned as your 'go-to' response to explain the value of any given item, using FAB will make your communication so much easier and consistent. No product or service will ever phase you again as this skill can be applied to any given situation and any product.

So long as you identify the Features, the Advantages and the Benefits of a given product or service and communicate them in that order your communication will be enhanced. Furthermore your client will connect at a far deeper level with what you're proposing as it will make sense to them. They'll get what it will do for them and if what it does for them links to their product and emotional needs they will be delighted that a solution is available. You'll have a very happy client and you'll also be on your way to a sale.

So let's break it down a little further.

What is a Feature?

A feature describes a product and/or service. In other words, what is this product or service?

SELLING
GENUINE YES

FEATURE
THIS IS A TOOTHBRUSH

ADVANTAGES

IT CLEANS TEETH AND GUMS!!

BENEFITS

- REDUCES CAVITIES
- FRESH BREATH
- NO STAINS

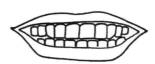

YES!

☑ THIS IS FOR ME!
☑ IT'S JUST WHAT I NEED!
☑ I'VE GOT TO HAVE IT NOW!
PLEASE CAN I BUY?

What is an Advantage?

An advantage describes what the product or service does. In other words, what does this product or service do?

What is a Benefit?

A benefit describes what's in it for the user. It describes the value to the user. In other words, why is this product or service great for the user?

So let's play around with this for a while.

Feature: this is a toothbrush.

Advantage: it helps to clean your teeth and gums.

Benefit: which means that you will have healthy teeth and gums,

which means that you will reduce getting cavities,

which means that you will have fresh breath,

which means that your teeth won't develop stains.

Let's take another Feature, Advantage and Benefit of a toothbrush.

Feature: these are the bristles on the toothbrush

Advantage: these bristles ensure that you can clean between your teeth.

Benefit: this means that you will release food and bacteria from between your teeth,

> which means that you will reduce inflammation and cavities,

> which means that you will have fresh breath, which means that…

> which means that…

Whenever you deliver the FAB – the Feature, the Advantage *which means that* the Benefit is x. Always link the advantage to the benefit by, *which means that.*

Using the FAB method to present your solution will ensure that key points are delivered to your client in a fresh, conversational and highly efficient manner. Your client will appreciate you putting it together for them in a coherent and straightforward manner. It is your job to help your client; using FAB really gets to the heart of the matter, and quickly. It is an enabler to engaging your client.

Recommended actions

This is important.

Having taken the time out to really understand what your client's needs are, it is now imperative to offer a solution that specifically meets those needs. If you don't have products and services that meet their needs, tell them. You'll be highly respected and your client is likely to recommend you to others as being honest and straightforward; qualities that travel well.

So this is the important bit: I strongly recommend that you make an extensive FAB list of every product or service that you have within your portfolio and put it in an easy to use format for yourself. This means that you will have all of the information that you require to hand. You will be more familiar with your products and services and this will give you greater confidence and certainty when you are with your clients.

This requires effort. As in Chapter 3, *Entering the Sale*, there will be a direct correlation between how much effort you put in and your sales results. This is a job that needs to happen prior to engaging with your client.

Until you are practiced and have mastered this skill, this will require effort on your part. Arguably people who have achieved mastery are often the ones that practice relentlessly in order to build their knowledge and fine-tune their skills. Do the work and you'll be rewarded. There are no short cuts to this. As a minimum, my recommendation is that you FAB the following topics and practise regularly.

- You
- Your Company – your Brand.

- Products

- Services

- Payment options

- Guarantees or Warranties

- After sales back-up and service

Depending on your sales environment and what it is that you're selling, there will certainly be many other topics to FAB.

Take some time out, consider them all because by knowing and practicing the Features, Advantages and Benefits in all areas of your business, and in the products and services that you offer, you will increase the quality of your presentation.

By using FAB, you will be far better placed to link all your clients' needs – both product and emotional needs.

It will help ensure that your presentation is appropriate, powerful and relevant. That will help you increase the level of client engagement, which means that your clients will have a superior sales experience by engaging with you. This nearly always leads to increased client satisfaction and increased sales conversion.

Presenting the Price

You've spent time presenting the features, advantages and benefits of each item you are proposing and each FAB relates and links to a specific client need. Now your client understands your recommended solution and how it meets each need they have. So, all that is left is to present the price.

Presenting the price in a methodical fashion allows your client to absorb the numbers and process what you are saying.

The products and services you offer will determine how you build your quotation — different environments lend themselves to slightly different point of sale situations. Retail environments, business to business settings, and selling in the home, will all have slightly different slants on the exact protocol at the point of sale. However, by methodically going through each line of your solution, quotation or estimate, by highlighting each product and/or service listed and reiterating the benefits of each product and/or service, you naturally conclude by confirming the price to your client.

This is the gross price; the full price, which does not include deductions for any special offers or local promotions you may have available from time to time. Should this be the case, once you have delivered the gross price to your client, you are then able to proceed with any deductions that may be available at that time.

Your client will then have the two elements of the quotation in front of them — the gross price and a promotional price.

For a special offer or promotion to be effective, it is likely that it will have a criterion that needs to be met, such as a time frame around the reduction in price or the delivery of the goods, or perhaps when a volume is purchased a particular item or service is added free of charge. Whatever the specifics, for a promotion to be effective there should always be some criteria that will need to be met by the client in order to qualify.

By delivering the gross price before deducting any special offers or promotions you are helping your client to process that the promotion is separate to the order.

Apart from periodic price increases and stock availability, the quotation is the quotation. As any special offer or promotion is likely to have a timeframe to its availability, deducting it immediately could cause confusion should your client not be in a position to proceed within the promotional timeframe.

Delivering the gross price separately to any current offer helps to avoid confusion, and avoiding confusion will support the value of being transparent at all times. It will further support you in your aim to deliver excellence and client satisfaction.

Apart from all of this, presenting your price in this manner will assist your client in their decision making and how they choose to proceed with their purchase. Your client will now have the gross price and the promotional price if there is one. Now all that is required is to cover the methods of payment; and let your client respond.

Please be aware at this stage nearly all clients will appreciate some time to absorb what you have just delivered to them; they will want and need to process the Gross price and, if relevant, the promotional price. This may take a few seconds or even a minute or two. Being respectful of this internal process is easily demonstrated by remaining quiet and letting your client process the information.

Rushing your client, distracting them by continuing to talk whilst they are in this thinking and processing stage will simply shut them down and they will not be able to reach a decision comfortably.

Your client will give you their response soon enough and you can then conclude the business by completing the relevant paperwork or payment.

Genuine Yes

Sales literature is frequently over populated with the topic of 'closing the sale' and frankly, in reality, much of it is nonsense. Often the nonsense is promoted by those who wish to create a mystery about selling and especially imply that there are tricks of the trade in terms of 'closing deals'.

Without a doubt there is an appropriate time to conclude the business, end the sales conversation or bring the client meeting to a close. In my experience it is seldom of value to start some massive closing process which alienates and deters most folk.

You can be led to believe that there are sales tricks that will ensure you never, ever leave a client without a 'sale'. That is not what I teach. That is not my experience of how you achieve wholehearted sales success. More often than not you would have to sell out for that method to be effective.

Furthermore it is my experience those sorts of tactics will drain and exhaust you; will exhaust, bore and irritate your client, and you may find that any sales that are miraculously achieved are quickly cancelled or returned once your client is lucky enough to escape from your sales pitch.

The simple but powerful truths are:

- Make the effort to understand the true needs of your client.

- Make the effort to understand what they want and what's important to them, both from product and emotional needs points of view.

- Be genuinely interested in your client's desired outcome.

- Be interested and make sure you understand the problems that need to be solved.

- Create a solution for you client with their specific needs being met.

- Deliver that solution using Features, Advantages, Benefits that link to each and every one of your client's needs.

- Cover the methods of repayment , if appropriate.

- And by simply doing a great job, you may actually find that they simply want to BUY!

Your job is to help your clients BUY – it is not to FLOG stuff.

With your open intention and attitude of investigating what problems need to be solved, and by covering the points above, your clients will more often than not want to proceed.

The question for a Genuine Yes

You will no doubt have a preferred method of proceeding with a sale. The administrative process will differ from business to business and the sales environment will also play its part. However, the one area in common will be turning client visits or client engagements into an agreement to proceed – in other words, a sale.

If you are confident that you have delivered value and have been a 'super' problem solver for your client then it is a very natural next step for you to respectfully assume that they will want to proceed.

Having a respectfully assumptive mind-set is probably one of the most positive traits you can have as a sales person but it will only be positively received by your client if you have authentically delivered value and excellence. Some clients could be irritated by an overly confident sales person but if you have conducted yourself in the manner we've explored throughout this book your client will appreciate the lengths you have gone to in order to deliver excellence and meet their specific needs.

That said, regardless of the great job you've done so far, one of the most common errors inexperienced, oh and by the way also experienced, sales people make is to forget to ask for the order.

If you get to this stage and do not ask for the order you will be leaving your client high and dry. This will seriously jeopardise the outcome and their level of satisfaction.

Most clients will expect you to show them or tell them how they can proceed. In other words, your client will expect you to 'ask' them for the order so that they can buy.

Bear in mind that, as most clients will be expecting this, if you don't actually ask for their business, they will simply drift into not going ahead with the purchase at that time. On your part this poor service delivery will not only lead to poor sales results but also poor client satisfaction. Not good. It makes perfect sense to conclude the business at the first visit should your client be happy to proceed.

Making sure that you feel comfortable asking for the order is part of your job.

Each of us will have a slightly different set of words, perhaps some preferred phrases which feel the most authentic for us individually. Identifying them and practising them regularly will help with delighting your clients and it will increase your sales conversion.

So the important question for you to answer right now is; what is your preferred way of asking your clients if they are ready to buy?

If you're happy with everything, shall I go and book that in for you?

I think we've got everything covered now so would you like me to wrap that up for you?

How do you feel about that? Are you ready to go ahead now?

What's your preferred way of asking that question?

Handling objections

First up, what is an objection?

An objection, in the context of a sales process, is often seen as a client demonstrating a barrier to proceeding with an order, or showing some level of resistance to make a commitment, or simply a lack of motivation to purchase.

This may be true, your client may actually be resisting making a purchase yet very often it is simply an unanswered question that needs to be addressed. A point of clarification or a slight misunderstanding that is sufficient to halt their desire to proceed with their purchase. When this situation arises, it is your job to ensure that everything is clarified and settled such that your client feels comfortable. They will not proceed if they don't.

After discussion, should they not wish to proceed at least you will have ascertained the real reasons why. Getting accurate feedback as to why a sale has not been achieved is extremely valuable feedback for you. Whenever this kind of hesitation or resistance occurs it's important that you establish what created it and, if at all possible, address it immediately.

Objection prevention

There are endless processes which can be applied to overcoming objections but for me nothing is as powerful as avoiding a client having an objection in the first place.

Essentially, your client will need to feel that they are making a good, positive and useful decision in order to feel comfortable that now is the right time to go ahead with your recommended solution. Consistently successful sales people tend to adopt the attitude of looking inward and are willing and prepared to take full responsibility for their client's hesitation and reluctance to proceed.

If at the point of completing the sale your client is hesitant or resistant to your recommended solution, it is wise to assume that you have missed something. Unless, of course, it is abundantly obvious as to why the prospect can't proceed – for example, awaiting an external event like planning permission for a building extension prior to being in a position to purchase the interior fitments. Or other real and tangible reasons why this sale will not complete now.

But you should be aware of these during the sales conversation as you established your client needs, so it shouldn't be a surprise to you and arguably therefore not actually an objection.

By adopting a mind-set of taking responsibility for the outcome of every visit, you will find that you very quickly become even better and more focussed at asking good quality questions. Without doubt, successful sales people are excellent at asking good quality questions. After all, it is through your questioning ability that you will have established your clients' needs, which will have enabled you to arrive at your proposed solution. Should your client not wish to proceed it is important to determine how to advance the conversation.

For example:

If your client says that the quotation is too expensive, it could mean that

- It's more money than they thought it was going to be.
- They haven't got enough money in their bank account to pay for this.
- They need to find a way of funding this project.
- They always like to 'get a deal' – they're wondering if they can get a better price from you.
- They may have a cheaper quote.
- They may be wondering if they can get it cheaper elsewhere.
- And 101 other thoughts could be going through their mind.

Without clarifying what is actually going through your client's mind you will be none the wiser and arguably will not be serving your client as you originally intended. Which is to help them find a good solution for whatever problem is presenting – be that finding the perfect sun tan lotion or purchasing components for aircraft.

Until you get clarification from your client, you will have no idea why they are not proceeding. Failure to get this level of clarity will mean that sales will go unprocessed, potential customers will become disappointed and dissatisfied, and you will leave the sales situation without any real knowledge of why your client did not purchase.

So get comfortable with the reality that throughout the dialogue with your client there will be times when you will want and need to get greater clarification. How else could you help them?

Seeking clarity will ensure that you can identify and adequately answer any outstanding questions, issues or objections your client may have, so that they can proceed with their decision to purchase.

This will support you in determining what the true problems or any perceived barriers to proceeding with the purchase are. It will help you clarify and understand any barriers, and in doing so will assist you to refine and solve them so that your client can proceed with ease. Not only will this make the sales process a pleasant experience for your client it will also increase sales conversion and reduce cancellations and returns.

How do you clarify?

- Listen:
  When you perceive that your client is reluctant to move forward, listen carefully as always, to what they are saying to you.

- Play back:
  Then play back your understanding of what your client has just said to you.

- Once your client has confirmed that you've understood fully, proceed to answer their question, query or concern.

There are two main categories that tend to require clarification.

1. Misunderstanding.

2. Perceived disadvantage.

Misunderstanding

If it is a misunderstanding, explain the facts so that clarity is achieved for your client.

For example:

Client: I don't want to get the kitchen installed until my children go back to school.

You: May I ask why that's important to you?

Client: I don't want to have all the disruption whilst the children are at home all day during the holidays.

You: May I ask, is that your only concern?

Client: Yes.

You: I understand, so what you're saying is that you don't want to have the disruption whilst the children are at home during their summer holidays. That's perfectly understandable; we can plan your installation now and get it booked in for a time that is convenient for you once your children are back at school. How does that sound to you?

Your client is happy, feels understood and actually is understood because you bothered to clarify. They can now relax knowing that everything is taken care of.

Perceived Disadvantage

This is when your client believes that there is some sort of disadvantage to them by proceeding.

You will need to firstly establish what your client perceived to be a disadvantage. Then your job is to put the perceived disadvantage into perspective for your client.

Client: I didn't realise that the kitchen installation would take two full days.

You: May I ask, is that a concern to you?

Client: Well yes, I don't want to be without hot water and kitchen facilities for forty-eight hours.

You: Is that your only concern?

Client: Yes.

You: Ok, I now understand your concerns that you thought you would be without any kitchen facilities and hot water for two full days. I understand how important that is to you with small children. So what may be useful to you is to know how long you'll be without these facilities. Although the installation will take up to two full days it is our practice to do whatever we can to get your kitchen operational at the end of the first day. So although the installation will take two days to complete, you should have a place to cook and you'll definitely have hot water at the end of day one.

Your client is now fully briefed and has the full facts. They will be more relaxed and feel a greater sense of certainty. Please always be mindful that the need of certainty is one of the emotional needs us human like to have fulfilled; especially when a situation appears to be out of our immediate control, like the installation of a new kitchen. Or purchasing any new product or service, no matter how small or large.

Once your client's concerns are allayed they'll be ready to proceed.

So what's the story with client objections or perceived objections?

You will deal with many mini objections throughout the sales conversation. It is inevitable that this will happen and should be considered positive as you come closer to understanding what your client's true needs are. How else could you help them?

As you focus on getting clarity during the sales call or on the shop floor you will be better placed to help your client to a greater and greater degree.

Ultimately, the most effective way to overcome any major objections is to simply avoid having any objections in the first place.

By using the skills you have to ask good quality questions, you will almost certainly create a deeper rapport with your client and avoid having any serious objections.

Follow Up

You will not sell to everyone. Sorry, folks, it's just the way it is.

However, do not get confused with what may initially appear to be a no sale. Some clients will need to reflect and some may need to involve others in the decision making process, so to assume that because a sale has not been achieved at the first meeting is short sighted and dangerous to your sales business. If you don't have a robust follow up process in place you will definitely say goodbye to clients and a superior sales conversion.

It is your job, not your client's, to follow up.

It would be a waste of valuable time, your clients and yours should you not ensure a robust follow up process is in place for clients who are, for whatever reason, unable to proceed and purchase on their initial approach – your initial sales visit or call.

Prior to concluding your first conversation be that a call or a visit, it is good practice to gain agreement from your client when you will call or re-visit. Generally speaking and dependant on your sales environment, at this stage, it will be an agreement to telephone the prospect at some point in the near future. However, it can occasionally be necessary to make a second appointment there and then; an appointment at a more suitable time for your client to go ahead and conclude the business.

Whatever you agree with your prospect MUST be adhered to – a capital MUST. Failure to call at an arranged time or date could easily lead to dissatisfaction which in turn may lose you the business and your reputation.

Apart from wanting to secure an order on your first visit, this time with your prospect will have been about many things. From a purely commercial point of view, you want their business. If at all possible, the goal is to secure the business on the first visit, but as previously discussed, this is not always possible or appropriate. So, if not on the first visit, the secondary goal becomes securing the business at some point in the future.

You will significantly reduce your chances of achieving this secondary goal should you not have a robust follow up process in place. Engaging with prospects is a multi-task and multi-layer interaction. Apart from the obvious desire to achieve a sale, it's about so much more than what initially meets the eye. You'll be wanting to build relationships. You'll want to demonstrate that you're genuinely interested in their desired outcome. You'll want your client to know that you're trustworthy; their interest is your interest in terms of helping them achieve their outcomes.

The key here is to deliver customer satisfaction *before* they have actually become a customer.

The benefits are far-reaching – it's about building your business now and for the future. Someone who doesn't buy from you today, may buy tomorrow and if impressed with you and the service you provide may recommend you to colleagues, friends and family for years to come. This is a very powerful source of enquiry/lead for you and your business.

During the time you have had with your client you will have earned their trust. To then simply not follow up on that conversation could damage that level of trust you've worked so diligently to create. Not following up religiously will very often prevent you and your business from securing their order at a later date.

Being open and building trust with your clients has been a theme from Chapter 1. LOVE SELLING is about how to sell *without* having to sell out. Following up in a robust fashion is all part of the conversation about Opening rather than just Closing.

Trust and Customer Satisfaction

It takes a long time to build trust and yet only one broken promise can lose it. In very busy times it may be useful to ask for assistance from your support team, but no matter what the circumstances, it is important to always ensure that follow up calls are given priority in your weekly schedule. Plan and make time for this activity. It is not a 'nice to have' add on or something that is only done when you are scratching around for a sale. It is a vital part of your successful sales process.

Trust and openness are the cornerstones of LOVE SELLING. Make it part of your sales discipline and you and your clients will be delighted with the outcome.

Chapter 9: BRINGING IT ALL TOGETHER

Where L-O-V-E synthesises with S-E-L-L-I-N-G

*'It is the set of our sails, not the direction of the wind,
that determines which way we will go.'*

Jim Rohn

So let's pull all of this together now. Let's take the LOVE philosophy and the SELLING process and synthesise the two.

The L-O-V-E philosophy is designed to support you so that you blossom into your most magnificent and successful self. It is the foundation of LOVE SELLING; in particular, it is the bedrock of how to sell without selling out.

L – O – V – E

Letting Go – Opening – Value – Evaluation

Letting Go:

Releasing any pre-conceived notions of who you thought you ought to be so that you can be the very best and authentic You.

I extend my heartfelt invitation to you to let go.

Let go of who you thought you were supposed to be, who you thought you were conditioned to be, what you thought others wanted you to be, what you thought you ought to be, and just be. Be you.

Breathe in; accepting that in your most authentic form you are the very best version of yourself. Magnificent and as perfect as you were intended to be.

Breathe out; with the knowing of whom you've yearned to be, who you deserve to be. Relax into being the shining light that you already are.

Opening:

To create in you the ability to be open to receive information without judgement, without prejudice and without outcome in mind.

Setting the intention to be open, truly open, is to create within you in any particular moment an empty vessel such that you can receive.

Receive without judgement, without prejudice, without outcome in mind. To be available to the information that is in front of you, to actively listen and to take in the energy and the needs of another in any given situation.

To experience the gift of being fully engaged and fully present in that moment.

Be brave and open yourself up, hear your soul's purpose and in doing so create a vast vessel in you that has space to hold the space for others. This is where service resides.

Value:

To give and add value freely.

'Thousands of candles can be lit from a single candle, and the life of the candle will not be shortened. Happiness never decreases by being shared.'

Buddha

If you make the commitment to always add value greater than any price tag you'll quickly find out that your life will be enriched in ways that are almost unimaginable. Give your client relationships the benefit of your knowledge, expertise and generosity of spirit.

Give the energy of fair exchange the chance to manifest itself within your sales life. It feels great, your clients will feel great and life and sales results will rub along even better.

Evaluation:

Get those numbers down. Get clear on what numbers are important for you and your business. Which metrics drive your business and why. And ultimately what you need to achieve in order for things to rock along nicely.

Whether you love numbers or not, be vigilant in your metrics. You'll feel supported, you'll have clarity, certainty will creep into the corners of your sales business and you'll reduce nasty shocks turning up when you least expect them. Do this regularly and you'll be in control of your sales and your business.

Be alert, stay focussed and above all be truthful with yourself – there are no short cuts to success. The metrics will keep your on track, so use them.

S – E – L – L – I – N – G

Setting Intentions:

Setting intentions for yourself and also for your client.

Whatever you chose to put your attention on and focus on will gain energy and grow. It's the Universal Law of Cause and Effect.

Follow the three steps to mastering your intention setting and let the magic emerge.

Global intentions; the large directional guideposts of your life. The big picture.

Time bound intentions; the time bound specifics that you want to nail. Your sales target, the key presentation, securing your ideal client. What are you going for?

In the moment intentions; the sales call, the client meeting or the 1,001 other 'in the moment' encounters that are important to you.

Decide what it is that you want, get really clear, prioritise, put in the work required and go for it in the full knowledge that the force of the Universe is with you.

Time management becomes easier, saying yes or no becomes so straightforward you start to wonder why it was ever an issue. The myriad of choices you are faced with become easier and business decisions are cut and dried. They either align with your intentions at some level, or they do not. Your consciousness steps up a level and your decision making becomes stronger and more purposeful. Of course you'll still be challenged from time to time; that's part of life, but you can be at choice in the most sublime way without carrying unnecessary guilt, regret or confusion.

Enter the Sale:

The necessary preparation in order to deliver excellence.

Entering the sale is about preparing to deliver excellence. Making sure whatever sales aids, materials, products, samples or point of sale you need to deliver excellence are ready, prepared and waiting to serve your client and support the sales process.

It's making sure that you are ready. Your mind-set is clear, clean and fresh. That your thinking is conducive to being open and in receive mode for your client. That you show up in the most aligned fashion to serve your client.

This is about taking respectful control of the time you have with your client so that you can offer the most productive experience for them. It's about making sure your client knows what to expect from the time you have together.

Learning:

Learning about your client so that you can serve with grace.

Learning is about fact finding. What does your client want and need? What's important to them? What's the implication of their needs not being met?

Asking good quality questions is your way of ensuring that you get to the heart of the matter so you can truly understand their needs, both product and emotional, and what may happen if those needs don't get met.

The only way to deliver excellence is to establish what your client needs, why they need it and what will happen if they don't have that need met. In order for your solution to be appropriate and ecological it will depend on you having insight to your client needs. Without this level of insight you'll run the risk of offering an inappropriate solution.

Listening:

Tuning into your higher self and your client.

One of the greatest gifts we can bestow on our fellow humans is to listen. Being heard is at the heart of human connection. So how can we do this in the most elegant and purposeful fashion?

We start by listening to ourselves first. We become silent in our own energy, quieten ourselves and become still. We then hear our soul's gentle, all powerful voice, directing us in our purpose. As we tap into the full force of our internal guidance, our knowing becomes clearer and clearer such that we start the process of internal peace. Once quietened and clear in our own purpose we are far better placed to help others achieve theirs.

I urge you to listen to you first. Really take time out to hear what your soul is searching for; what and who you are and yearning to be. If you are prepared to listen to your soul you'll open up the pathway so that you can listen to others at a far deeper level. You'll be in a position to serve in the most spectacular way. You'll be free to connect in ways you probably thought were previously unavailable to you. Compassion and empathy will be your guide posts; for yourself and others. Relationships will flourish and life, and sales, will be so much more joyful.

Then listening to your clients will be easy. You'll hold the space so that you are able to understand exactly what it is that they want and need, and what's important to them and help them achieve it.

Involve:

The energy of connection and collaboration.

How does your non-verbal communication align, or not, with your verbal communication? Whatever you do, does it match the spirit of what you're saying? Does your non-verbal communication support or detract from your verbal communication?

We unconsciously gain, build and maintain rapport with those with whom we have a good relationship. It's our job to make sure that we do this with everyone with whom we engage in a sales environment. Whilst staying true to our values and respectful of those of our clients, it remains our job to meet the client where they're at. We cannot realistically expect the client to make that journey towards us.

Rapport is an enabler to good communication and we must take that lead. What's motivating our client? What's driving their behaviour now in this moment and with regards to this particular purchase? What do they want? What do they not want?

Establish this and you'll be well on your way to ensuring that you understand their needs. Meeting those needs is your job.

Needs:

Establishing what your client needs is central to understanding what they want and what's important to them.

Understanding your clients' needs, and I mean really getting to a clear understanding of both product and emotional needs, is the greatest service you can bestow on your client.

Taking it up a notch and understanding what the implications will be for your client should they not have their needs met, is the only way you'll be able to deliver service excellence. It's the heart of your job.

Genuine Yes:

Creating a safe and appropriate reason for your client to buy.

Presenting your solution in a format that is easy to understand and delivers value to the client is imperative. Using the Features, Advantages and Benefit format does just that. It quickly and conversationally gives your client the low down on what's in it for them.

People only buy what a product or service gives them – or delivers to them. Using FAB elegantly does just this. FAB can be used to present anything from the many benefits one would gain from using a toothbrush, through to after sales back up service. There are no limits to where FAB can be used to present in a productive way.

Presenting the price, asking for the order, handling objections are all part of the sales process. Once you've fully understood what your client wants and needs and why it's important to them, you'll understand the implications of them not fulfilling those needs with a product or service.

When you link each element of your solution to exactly how it will meet their needs your client's problems are solved. All that's left to do is to ask for the order and proceed with whatever the next steps are in your business. Whether that's wrapping up the products and putting them in a pretty carrier bag, completing an order form, or calling through to your office to book a delivery, your client will be pleased, relieved and delighted that you have helped them find what they were looking for.

For any client who isn't ready or able to proceed, the go to position is to gain agreement for the next contact point and follow up. This is always done prior to concluding the current sales conversation. Having diarised this, it will be your priority to meet that agreement as promised.

L-O-V-E S-E-L-L-I-N-G

L-O-V-E S-E-L-L-I-N-G is about service and delivering excellence. It's about being the very best version of yourself and committing to delivering the very best for your clients.

Follow the L-O-V-E S-E-L-L-I-N-G philosophy and process and there's a strong possibility that you'll fall in love with selling.

Before you know it, you'll find yourself growing and developing what you already know. You'll almost certainly expand, and your capacity to grow will grow even more. When you set intentions they'll start to get bigger, they may be braver and they'll definitely be more aligned to who you truly are. The fun of being in sales and in service will delight you. It'll easily become your most enjoyable activity and your energy will radiate and shine.

That's where the magic is. The energy of loving what you do is wonderfully powerful for others to witness and they'll want to be be part of it too. You'll find it bouncing back at you and your life expression will step up a notch.

My wish for you is that you achieve whatever it is that you wish for yourself.

One thing I know for sure is this.

When we choose fear, we constrict, we shrink, we panic, we under deliver, and we slide backwards into smaller and smaller versions of ourselves. We diminish, solutions become harder to find. Life becomes difficult and challenges appear insurmountable. We find our version of hell which is often dark, lonely and scary.

But when we choose love, we choose a pathway that expands. People and places conspire to help and support us. We expand, we deliver, we include, we embrace, and we grow into the very best version of ourselves. We become brave, we over deliver, solutions pop up as if by magic, we soar and life is fulfilling and meaningful.

We find our version of peace and joy.

I found mine in LOVE SELLING – it is my hope that this book helps you to do so too.

Andrey

x

Acknowledgements

I have complete certainty that this book wouldn't have seen the light of day had it not been for a number of people who were generous enough to help and guide me, both directly and indirectly. Not only in the actual process, but also in their generous support and loving encouragement along the way.

I originally thought that it would be a rather romantic process; one where I'd be sitting on my balcony looking at the view of the sea, drinking good coffee and getting all creative whilst popping out my first book. It didn't quite work like that.

For me, it only works by being surrounded by some pretty special people who are not only talented and gifted but also kind and supportive, yet are prepared to be equally challenging of my work and demanding of excellence when required. And then there are those very special few who have always been willing and prepared to encourage me, no matter what, to fulfil my potential so that I can help others to do the same. I'd like to thank you all.

First up: Joe Gregory and Lucy McCarraher and the team at Rethink Press. Joe for his fabulous flow of creativity, inspirational coaching and ad hoc downloads of pure bloody genius. Lucy for gently yet firmly keeping me on track, giving me structure, context and her eagle eye in refining and editing. You've both taken the 'daunting' out of writing a book and I look forward to working with you again on book number two.

To Tim Kenning – you took my words and created magical illustrations in front of my eyes. Thank you for adding this delightful dimension.

A heartfelt thank you to those of you who I worked alongside in my corporate career, whether as a direct report, sales manager or sales force. I especially want to thank those at British Gas and Sharps Bedrooms. Your stellar support when we worked alongside each other gave me the courage to be much braver than I would have been otherwise, and the fact that you were prepared to seriously challenge me at times forced me to grow. I might add that sometimes that 'growth' was a little faster than I had intended but I'm hugely grateful for the time we worked together. I shall remember it fondly always.

To my clients – you have proven beyond any doubt that intention-setting works. Thanks to you all, many of the intentions I have set for myself and my business have already manifested themselves in reality. I love working with you all and I appreciate and thank you for putting your faith in me; it is a privilege and a delight to work with you all.

A special thanks to Richard Harpin, Founder and CEO of HomeServe plc who, without realising it, has been a significant part of my inspiration to write this book.

To my students and mentees: You never fail to motivate me with your willingness to do whatever it takes to get to be your greatest version. Thank you for your energetic participation and for helping me to grow as a teacher.

To my many teachers and influencers: Especially Dr Susi Strang-Wood, Dr John Demartini, Marie Forleo and B-School, La Rue Eppler, Dharma Gaynes and Marja Vraets-Guliker. You have all created in me a depth of joy through your work and teaching. Words do not adequately reflect my gratitude. Suffice it to say that the richness you have brought into my life through your classes have expanded me in ways which have been truly game changing. Thank you.

To the guys at The Sales Academy: Especially my mentor and friend Steve Clark who has tirelessly supported and encouraged me over the years, and who always manages to add a dose of deliciously dry humour to any stressful situation.

To my extended family: Especially Liz Hill and La Rue Eppler.

Liz who since junior High School has been a sister figure and confidant to me, who later became a wonderful Godmother to my son and above all has been a friend who has faithfully been by my side through thick and thin. Your kindness and unrelenting belief in me has pushed me to go for it even when I really didn't want to.

La Rue who started as my teacher, became a dear friend and now a spirit sister. Whose loving support, wise guidance and gentle kindness knows no bounds.

I love you both dearly.

To my coaches: Brian Kiell and Steph Burton.

Although I have known and worked with Brian for many years, when he agreed to become my business coach a few years ago I never realised that I was about to gain a friend and a business confidant. He has been the voice of sense, the gentle but firm prod in my ribs to get out there and do my work. I have absolute certainty that his coaching has, without doubt, been the difference that has made the difference to me. His ability to allow me to tell my stories, sometimes at ridiculous length, and yet always bring me back to reality without a bump is remarkable. I owe him so much, both personally and professionally. Thank you.

Steph Burton my energy coach. Over the past couple of years, the role of energy coach has melded and developed into that of deep friendship and sisterhood. The only way to describe this deeply spiritual and insightful healer, whose sublime insights into esoteric matters are as sharp as her energy coaching, is that she is a crazy French woman whose leisure pursuits include karate and other martial arts. I should also mention that this extends to pretty much any serious contact sport like kick boxing *et al*. I kid you not – I couldn't make this up. By the way, it's perhaps also worth mentioning that I tend to wince at any kind of physical fighting; so ours is an interesting partnership. Her approach is gentle and kick-ass at the same time. Her energy coaching has meant that my work has taken on a dimension that was previously lacking. Always kick-ass, always with deep love, her support has transformed me. Thank you sista.

But it is the two men in my life that I have the most to be thankful for.

Jerry Moore, who I first met in 1997 as my boss, became a colleague and friend, and all these years later is now my life partner, business partner, sparring partner and 'bestest' mate. He will irritatingly claim that any success I've had or will ever have, any achievement, any good thought, word, act or deed that I perform is and will always be due to his phenomenal guidance and teaching. This is of course, false. However this belief of his, this false belief, will give a brief insight to the life we share.

His dry sense of humour is interspersed with great kindness and a plethora of unusual one-liners which he considers to be motivational.

One year when I decided to take a break from working to reflect and consider what it was that I really wanted to do with my business life, my usual income inevitably dipped. In true Jerry style, he announced that he may have to 'let me go' if my desire to find myself was to last much longer. That led to me starting a business which I now love. Such is our relationship of push and pull. Irritatingly, it seems to produce good results.

On a serious note, without this man so much of what I've been able to achieve would have passed me by and have simply been unattainable. It's probably not that easy, living with someone like me who believes in pots of gold at the end of rainbows, unicorns, and who loves to dream big. But he has allowed me the space, in fact at times has specifically created the space for me to be me. He is big hearted enough to be comfortable with me finding my true expression and has supported me both emotionally and financially when I had the need and the urge to follow my dreams. He 'gets' me and for that I have deep gratitude and love him to bits.

It is without question, though, that for me the most important person on this planet and in my life is my son Stuart Chapman. Each and every day since his arrival I have thanked God that he chose me to be his mom in this lifetime.

Although my son, he has at times parented me and as an adult has become a best friend, a coach, a confidant, the most loyal supporter and a fierce motivator. He packs a mean punch when it comes to forcing me to acknowledge what is possible should I put my mind to it. He gives me more in terms of motivation than he realises. He is my driver, the main reason I step up to the plate and is also a great leveller in terms of what I believe I can and cannot control.

I believe that we have travelled many lifetimes together and will continue to do so again. I love him with all my heart.

I consider myself to be a fortunate person. I'm very aware of the incredible support and at times what I consider to be the exquisite challenge that I have in my life. For me, a good life is about having both support and challenge and striving for the middle ground of attaining a place of balance between the two whenever possible.

It is with heartfelt gratitude that I thank you all for presenting both.

The Author

From the shop floor to the boardroom, Audrey has created many years of sales success and taught many others to achieve the same.

Throughout her corporate career, which spanned a couple of decades, she earned the reputation of significant over-achievement whilst successfully delivering change in complex sales environments.

In 2011 she left corporate employment, started a freelance career and in 2015 founded The Sales Resolution.

Working with organisations from start-ups through to plcs, her success has been rooted in her ability to create sales openness combined with a razor sharp ability to get clarity about how sales functions align with the wider business and their customers.

Described by her colleagues and clients as inspirational and innovative, Audrey specialises in stimulating sales success for individuals and creating outstanding sales teams.

Students, coaching clients and mentees flourish under her tutelage whilst corporate clients enjoy immediate success from the bespoke programs she designs, manages and delivers for them.

At the heart of Audrey's unique approach lies her certainty in the belief that it is 'Opening' rather than 'Closing' that leads to a successful sales life. Time and time again she has proven that it is in this sacred space that the individual sales person, the client and the business all remain whole and where sustainable sales success resides.

Audrey is Director of The Sales Resolution, an accomplished trainer, coach and speaker.

www.thesalesresolution.co

f @thesalesresolution

🐦 @Love_Selling1

in audrey-chapman

26642651R00105

Printed in Great Britain
by Amazon